This Wild Darkness

This Wild Darkness

The Story of My Death

Harold Brodkey

Metropolitan Books

Henry Holt and Company ▪ New York

Metropolitan Books
Henry Holt and Company, Inc.
Publishers since 1866
115 West 18th Street
New York, New York 10011

Metropolitan Books™ is an imprint of
Henry Holt and Company, Inc.

Published in Canada by Fitzhenry & Whiteside Ltd.
195 Allstate Parkway, Markham, Ontario L3R 4T8.

Portions of this book appeared in
The New Yorker in different form.

Library of Congress Cataloging-in-Publication Data
Brodkey, Harold.
This wild darkness: the story of my death / Harold Brodkey. — 1st ed.
p.   cm.
1. Brodkey, Harold—Last years. 2. Authors, American—20th century—
Biography. 3. AIDS (Disease)—Patients—United States—Biography.
I. Title.
PS3552.R6224Z474 1996   96-16518
813'.54—dc20   CIP
                                                                    [B]

ISBN 0-8050-4831-6

Henry Holt books are available for special promotions
and premiums. For details contact: Director, Special Markets.

First Edition—1996

Designed by Betty Lew

Printed in the United States of America
All first editions are printed on acid-free paper. ∞

1   3   5   7   9   10   8   6   4   2

For Ellen, my light . . .

I want to thank Tina Brown and Michael Naumann and David Godwin for their loyalty and generosity in all matters concerning Harold and his work. I take this liberty because no one knows better than I what his life would have been like without them; or without Kim Heron, his editor during these last hard-won years.

—*Ellen Schwamm Brodkey*

I don't see the point of privacy.
Or rather, I don't see the point of leaving testimony
in the hands or mouths of others.

—*H.B.*, June 1993

This Wild Darkness

I have AIDS. I am surprised that I do. I have not been exposed since 1977, which is to say that my experiences, my adventures in homosexuality took place largely in the 1960s and '70s, and back then I relied on time and abstinence to indicate my degree of freedom from infection and to protect others and myself.

At first, shadows and doubts of various kinds disturbed my sleep, but later I felt more certainty of safety. Before AIDS was identified, I thought five years without noticeable infection would indicate that one was without disease. When AIDS was first identified, five years was held to indicate safety. That changed. Twenty years now is considered a distance in time that might indicate safety, but a slight number of AIDS cases are anomalous; that is, the delay in illness is not explicable within the assumed rules, even under the most careful, cynical investigation. It doesn't matter much. I have AIDS. I have had *Pneumocystis carinii* pneumonia, which almost killed me. Unlikely or not, blood test, T-cell count, the fact that it was *Pneumocystis* means I have AIDS and must die.

There it is. At the time I was told, I didn't even believe I had pneumonia. I thought it was literary exhaustion, and age, and bad flu-bronchitis—the death-urgency brought on by finishing a book, what I called the Venice book, *Profane Friendship*. When the piece of journalism I was working on, a piece about the Academy Awards for *The New Yorker*, was done and scheduled to go to press, I went to see my doctor, Barry Hartman. I wasn't that familiar with him yet that I easily called him Barry. He was my new internist, a specialist in infectious diseases. He had taken over the practice of the doctor I'd had before. He looked at the X rays and at how thin I was and said it might be AIDS and *Pneumocystis*, and I pooh-poohed him. Because of my wife, Ellen Schwamm,

I agreed to the HIV test, but I refused to go to the hospital. And Barry said he might be wrong.

He said he would telephone with the test results. I said he shouldn't worry about it. I wasn't tense.

I went home, went to bed, took the general-spectrum antibiotic Barry had prescribed, and in bed went through the Academy Awards piece with the fact-checker on the phone. And I suffered with flu-bronchitis and fever but not with foreboding. I had some nervousness about the test, since you never know what surprises God has up *His* sleeve, destiny's sleeve. But not much. It had been a very long time. I didn't even have that lapsed awareness one can get when sick, *You goddamned fool, why did you stay up so late?* I didn't have that kind of contrition.

But by the next evening I was so much worse that I could not find a balance point in the gusts of unpleasant sensation. I don't remember feeling panicky, but I felt so sick I was uneasy about death (from illness, at least) for the first time in my life. Ellen was treating me with an unyielding attention and a kind of sweetness, without any noticeable flicker of independence or irony. She had never once been like that with me, even sexually. You'd have to know her to know how rare any state other than autonomy is for her. It was strange how the illness kept getting heavier and more settled by the hour, with a kind of muffled rapidity. Again and again, it thudded to a level of horrendousness, consolidated that, and then thuddingly sank to a worse level still. Nothing was stopping the process of strangulation. I kept putting on a front for Ellen, or trying to, until, in a kind of extreme inward silence, nothing was working. The weird, choked dizziness didn't moderate or waver; I found I could not breathe at all, even sitting up.

I gave in. I said we'd better get to the hospital. The ambulance people came, and I whispered to them that I could not walk or sit up. Or breathe. They went down for a gurney and oxygen. Breathing through a tube in my nose and motionless and sheeted on a gurney, I was wheeled through our apartment and into the elevator and across the lobby, past the doorman, onto the sidewalk, into the air briefly, and then into the ambulance. This is how my life ended. And my dying began.

When Barry said I had AIDS, I said I didn't believe him. He said, "Believe me." At that instant, I was having such difficulty breathing that I hardly cared. I was embarrassed and shamed that the people who cared for me in the hospital would have to take special precautions to protect themselves. Then, as the fever went down, I suppose my pride and sense of competition took over. When someone from Social Services showed up to offer counsel, I found that bothersome, although the counselor was a very fine person, warm and intelligent. I suppose I was competitive with or antagonistic toward the assumption that now my death would be harder than other deaths, harder to bear, and that the sentence to such death and suffering was unbearable. I didn't find it so. I didn't want to find it so.

Ellen says that when we were first told, on a Monday, she sat in the one chair in the hospital room. To prove that she is actually remembering in the Brodkey mode, according to Brodkey theories and method, she says that Barry leaned against the windowsill with his arms folded while he told us. And that the weather was warm. And that I was strangely jovial and reasonable. She says I was heroic and completely in charge, and that I surprised her by agreeing *agreeably* to being treated for *Pneumocystis* rather than asking for sedation and being allowed to die. I remember Barry propping himself with one arm on the sill and then refolding his arms and saying, "You *have* AIDS," and holding his pose and staring at me.

Yet these first moments in which I consciously felt the reality of having AIDS are hazy, slippery, and return to me in different coverings. I was in New York Hospital, and in a private room—itself a sign of possibly having AIDS-related tuberculosis, to go from the emergency

room to a private room—and still hardly able to breathe
even with oxygen, and I had a high fever, and I was
drugged, though not as heavily as later. I was breathing
oxygen through a tube from a tank and I was attached to
an IV. I wasn't in a condition of vanity and yet I was—I
was worried about Ellen's opinion of me. I suppose this is
a male way of worrying about her feelings, her reactions,
without quite worrying about her.

The fever moved in acid waves. Some sort of final cas-
tration, real helplessness, felt very close. I could see
nothing to do about it. A display of manner, a touch of
William Powell, of Huckleberry Finn with the bed as the
raft, was like a broken piece of salvage to me.

I heard Ellen say something to Barry, ask him something about what was going to happen, and he said that
after the *Pneumocystis* cleared up I had the possibility of a
few years of life.

And I said, "But it will be embarrassing." The
stigma. Incontinence. (Would I have to wear a diaper?)
Blindness. He said the good years were quite good, were
livable.

In the confused, muddled velocities of my mind was
an editorial sense that this was wrong, that this was an
ill-judged element in the story of my life. I felt too conceited to have this death. I was illogical, fevered, but my

mind still moved as if it were a rational mind—the mind, everyone's mind, is forever unstill, is a continuous restlessness like light, even in sleep, when the light is inside and not outside the skull. I took inside me the first stirrings of acknowledgment of AIDS, not with the arching consciousness with which I try to write fiction—I didn't feel that isolation—but with a different sense of aloneness. And maybe I felt the wretchedness in Ellen. Maybe I was sensitive to what I had, so to speak, done to her now.

Part of what is basic in my life is how I show off for her. Somehow, sadly, that evening I was getting it wrong. I was wheezing too much, and Ellen kept indicating that I shouldn't try to talk unnecessarily. She was scared shitless. She was deep into her bravery tactic—almost trembling with it. Only in a memory which resurrects the fever, in that full memory, do I see her, strong-eyed, polite-voiced, and feel her leaning over me as if to protect me with her small frame. She said to me later that she had had the conviction that it was over for us, both of us—that she, too, must be infected, all things considered. Nothing for us, of us, would survive this devastation. But she said nothing of it then. She is often indirect; she frequently lies to me because I bully her in a lot of ways; she is quick, tactically quick.

She says she thought then that we would die together, both of us—commit suicide simultaneously— in a few months, when everything was in order. But she didn't want me to leave her now, not this abruptly. Most of us who know Ellen know her as a fine-boned tyrant who looks a bit like a small Garbo. Her hair is gray, and she has never had a face-lift. She is of interest physically still—neatly formed and stylized, like the stopper of an expensive perfume bottle. She is incredibly willful, and she is my human credential. People think she is good-looking and trustworthy and sensible, whatever they think of me. It seemed clear from how Barry and the harried nurses acted that they saw her in that way. They all trusted her judgment and her will, not mine.

I remember not wanting to be an exploitative fool in her eyes by asking her to nurse me through a terminal disease, and one with a sexual stigma. I wondered if she would despise me. I knew a woman once who'd had a good marriage, unmistakably so, within limits, and whose husband, a clever banker, fell ill and impressed everyone with how hard he fought to be himself again, to get well again. That woman once said in my hearing, "I wish he would give up." His struggle went on for so long, and so dominated everything, that it was killing her. And he was hardly alive except as a will to struggle.

And then, lying in that room, I saw it differently: after all, death—and AIDS—are a commonplace. "Big deal," I said. That didn't lighten anyone's face. "Jesus Christ," I said. "What a mess." Barry said something about tranquilizers and counseling to help with the shock and despair, and natural grief. "I'm OK," I said, and went on grandly, "Look, it's only death. It's not like losing your hair or all your money. I don't have to live with this."

I wanted to make them laugh. I wanted them to admire me, it's true, but I also wanted Ellen to stop that inward shaking, and I was afraid to say, "Christ, what have I done?" or "Look what's happened to me" or "It's all my fault." I have an odd cowardice toward grief. I would just as soon suffer without it. The two of them were watching me, ready to sympathize and comfort. Ellen turned to Barry, who was disapproving. Or worried. "We can help when the despair hits; we have drugs," he told her.

I was only thinly and artificially conscious anyway. I suppose I had made up my mind to try not to be humiliated, and that involved my not being pitiable to these two people, the only two people I would see with any regularity for the next eight weeks. And, you see, a traumatized child, as I was once, long ago, and one who recovers, as I did, has a wall between him and pain and despair, between him and grief, between himself and beshitting himself. That's the measure for me— handling the whole weight of my life in relation to polite bowels. The rest is madness, rage, humiliation.

Again, the fevered cresting memory pulls me back in, to that moment when I think it was that the future had suddenly vanished for me, had become a soft, deadened wall. Back there at the beginning, the end, when Barry told me flat-out that I had AIDS, I didn't feel it, although I also saw that denial was futile. Barry was not even remotely real to me at that point. He was merely a conductor, a lightning rod of medical error. I still didn't believe he was a good doctor; that would come later. The framework of the self wasn't changed by the words, the general feeling of its being my body and its having been my body all my life didn't dissolve, as it would in a few days. I had no sense of gestating my death.

Ellen says that she hung back and expected me to be violent psychically, and to want death immediately once I had accepted the diagnosis. Well, that was true. But I was also afraid of death, of my own final silence.

And I was ashamed toward her, and angry at her. She does not steadily believe that I love her—it is one of her least endearing traits to expect proof at unreasonable intervals. And what is love? My measure of it is that I should have died to spare her. Her measure is for us to be together longer.

I thought I could feel myself being suffocated second by second. What was strange was that all sense of presence, all sense of poetry and style, all sense of idea left me. It was gone, with not one trace, one flicker remaining. I had a pale sense of the lost strength it would take to think or feel a metaphor, and of how distant it was from me. Everything was suffocation and the sentence of death, the termite-like democracy and chemical gusts of malaise and heat, of twisting fever, and the lazy but busy simmering of the disease in me. Everything outside me was Ellen's breath and the color of the walls in the dim light and was the hospital noises and the television set on its wall mount and a ticking slide of the moments.

And nothing was a phrase or seed of speech, nothing carried illumination in it, nothing spoke of meaning, of anything beyond breath. Attentive to nothing but breath, perhaps in my dying I was alive in a real and complete way, a human way, for the first time after ten or fifteen years of hard work. I lay awake in an almost bright amusement. Did you ever, as a child, play alone in a large cardboard box that a refrigerator came in? Or work alone in a large room? Or at night, when everyone else was asleep? Whatever I say now applies to feelings inside such a box, the box I'm in. No one can possibly know the power of feeling I project inside my carton.

For the next two weeks, the world and all other issues would be omitted. We were two people alone in a hospital room. We allowed no visitors. We had two weeks of near-silence with each other and my increasing helplessness. I tended to tangle the IV and misplace the oxygen tube. As I started to say earlier, I could feel no sensible interest in the future. The moments became extraordinarily dimensionless—not without value but flat and a great deal emptier. When you learn you're fatally ill, time becomes very confusing, perhaps uninteresting, pedestrian. But my not caring if I lived or died hurt Ellen. And I was grateful that I could indulge my cowardice toward death in terms of living for her.

I remember her arriving back at the hospital that first night after four horrible hours at home, in our apartment alone, racked by waking nightmare. She arrived soon after it got light and had a bed for herself moved into my hospital room.

She said, in an averted way, "I want more time with you."

And I said, from within my flattened world, "You're nuts. It isn't that much fun to live. Now. And you know it." I sighed. "But if that's what you want . . ."

"I do," she said.

I don't want to be defensively middle class about this, but it was a middle-class decision I made, nothing glorious, to try to go ahead and have AIDS, live with it, for a while. I felt the doom was bearable. Also I was not, am not, young. I am not being cut down before I have had a chance to live. Most important, I was not and am not alone. I am embarrassed to be ill and to be ill in this way, but no one yet has shown disgust or revulsion. I expected it. To the interns AIDS is medically boring now (and I did not have a recondite opportunistic infection, but the most common one), and outside the hospital it arouses, at least in New York, sympathy and curiosity. I do get the feeling I am a bit on show, or rather my death and moods are. But so what?

Barry, who is very able and very experienced, is surprised that I am not more depressed. He says cheerfully that I am much more upset than I realize. He credits some of the medicines with shielding me, my mood, and warns me that severe unhappiness is coming, but so far it hasn't come. I have resisted it, I suppose. And my wife is with me every moment. I feel cut off from old age, it's true, but that's not like someone young feeling cut off from most of his or her possible life.

To be honest, the effort of writing, and then my age,

and the oppressive suffocation of the illness itself, and my sad conviction of the *important* validity of my ideas (of what my work presents), and my hapless defense of that work had so tired me that I was relieved by the thought of death. But I also wanted to make a defiant gesture at AIDS. So it became a matter of contrary style. The disease and its coercions (like all coercions) were contemptible. I figured that later on I would make meek friends with it while it killed me, but not just yet. This performance startled Ellen, who assumed for a while that I would break down all at once. (I am not sure what I myself expected, but it happened quietly and almost secretly. Ellen would describe her own reaction differently.)

She left her husband for me. She walked out on everything. No one backed her but her children. We have had fifteen years together so far. Some of those years were quite tense, with public attacks that were a bit on the vicious side. Things hadn't been all that smooth between me and her children or me and my daughter. Some of those years had been unbelievably hard. One of her sons had been very ill, and the public attacks hadn't let up even while the boy was sick. That first night in the hospital she tried to make up her mind that it was all worth it, but such matters are hard to resolve when you're alone. She tells me that she felt terrified and lost. She insists that she regrets nothing. This is her discipline and self-assertion when, openly or not, one is in her charge—what she can give you, the power to give, is the chosen motto of her personal constitution. She will be omnipresent because she has to be in order to comfort you within her standards of bestowing comfort. One keeps stumbling on the rocky ground of this half-hidden omnipotence, which is the governing element of any household she runs, any love affair she is in. It is half of every kiss she gives.

Ellen's secularity is combined with a sense of miracle and of meaningful destiny. She absorbs bad news but it is advisable to offer her hope, a way out, a line of inquiry. She is incredibly self-willed, as I've said, incredibly full of getting-on-with-it. Yet there was nowhere to go. She indulged me, followed my uncertain lead. She cried when she learned that she was clear of the virus; she said it depressed her to be so separated from me. And I felt that if I had AIDS, she had the right, perhaps the duty, to leave me; my having that disease suspended all contracts and emotions—it was beyond sacrament and marriage. It represented a new state, in which, in a sense, we did not exist. What we were had been dissolved, as if by radiation or the action of an acid. Perhaps the *sacrament* remained, but it was between her and her beliefs now: care wasn't, in my view, owed to me anymore. I wasn't me, for one thing. And she had suffered enough.

As for me, I would find a way through. I had rarely been ill as a child or an adult, but when I was, it was always serious, nearly fatal. I have been given up by my doctors three times in my life and for a few minutes a fourth time. This time is more convincing but otherwise it is not an unfamiliar or unexplained territory.

I was a hypochondriac, but for a good reason—I could take no medicine, none at all, without extreme, perverse, or allergic reactions. Essentially I never got sick. I was gym-going, hike-taking, cautious, oversensitive to the quality of the air, to heat and cold, noise and odors, someone who felt tireder more quickly than most people because of all these knife-edge reactions, someone who was careful not to get sick, because my allergic reactions to medicines made almost any illness a drastic experience.

I had an extremely stable baseline of mood and of mind, of mental *landscape*. Well, that's gone; it's entirely gone. From the moment my oxygen intake fell to about fifty percent and the ambulance drivers arrived in our apartment with the gurney and the oxygen, from that moment and then in the hospital until now, I have not had even one moment of physical stability. I am filled off-and-on with surf noises as if I were a seashell, my blood seems to fizz and tingle. I have low and high fevers. For a day I had a kind of fever with chills and sweats but with body temperature *below* normal, at ninety-six degrees. I have choked and had trouble breathing. I have had pleuritis, or pleurisy, in my right lung, an inflammation of the thoracic cavity which feels like a burning stiffness of the muscles and which hurt like hell if I coughed, moved suddenly, or reached to pick something up.

And, of course, one can die at any moment or discover symptoms of some entirely new disease. My life has changed into this death, irreversibly.

But I don't *think* the death sentence bothers me. I don't see why it should more than before. I have had little trouble living with the death-warrant aspect of life until now. I never denied, never hysterically defined the reality of death, the presence and idea of it, the inevitability of it. I always knew *I* would die. I never felt invulnerable or immortal. I felt the presence and menace of death in bright sunlight and in the woods and in moments of danger in cars and planes. I felt it in others' lives. Fear and rage toward death for me is focused on resisting death's soft jaws at key moments, fighting back the interruption, the separation. In physical moments when I was younger, I had great surges of wild strength when in danger—mountain climbing, for instance—or threatened in a fight or by muggers in the city. In the old days I would put my childish or young strength at the service of people who were ill. I would lend them my willpower, too. Death scared me some, maybe even terrified me in a way, but at the same time I had no great fear of death.

As with other children, when I was very young, death was interesting—dead insects, dead birds, dead people. In a middle-class, upper-middle-class milieu, everything connected to real death was odd, I mean in relation to pretensions and statements, projects and language and pride. Death seemed softly adamant, an undoing, a rearrangement, a softly meddlesome and irresistible silence. It was something some boys I knew and I thought we ought to familiarize ourselves with. Early on, and also in adolescence, we had a particular, conscious will not to be controlled by fear of death—there were things we would rather die than do. To some extent this rebelliousness was controlled; to some extent, we could choose our dangers, but not always. All this may be common among the young during a war; I grew up during the Second World War, when confronting un-natural death became a sad routine. And a lot was dependent on locality, and social class, on the defense of the sexual self or the private self against one's father or in school.

Having accepted death long ago in order to be physically and morally free to some extent, I am not crushed by this final sentence of death, at least not yet, and I don't think it is denial. Why should it be different now? Ought I to crack up because a bluff has been called? I am sick and exhausted, numbed and darkened, by my approximate dying a few weeks ago from *Pneumocystis*, and consider death a silence, a silence and a privacy and an untouchability, as no more reactions and opinions, as a relief, a privilege, a lucky and graceful and symmetrical silence to be grateful for. The actual words I used inwardly read ambiguously when written out: *it's about time* for silence.

I'm sixty-two, and it's ecological sense to die while you're still productive, die and clear a space for others, old and young. I didn't always appreciate what I had at the time, but I am aware now that accusations against me of being lucky in love were pretty much true and of being lucky sexually, also true. And lucky intellectually and, occasionally, lucky in the people I worked with. I have no sad stories about love or sex.

And I think my work will live. And I am tired of defending it, tired of giving my life to it. I have been a figure of aesthetic and literary controversy, the object of media savagery and ridicule, also at times of praise. I have been sniped at in the gossip-flood of New York and Europe and used up enormous amounts of energy dealing with it all. But I have liked my life. I like my life at present, being ill. I like the people I deal with. I don't feel I am being whisked off the stage or murdered and stuffed in a laundry hamper while my life is incomplete. It's my turn to die—I can see that that is interesting to some people but not that it is tragic. Yes, I was left out of some things and was cheated over a lifetime in a bad way, but who isn't and so what? I had a lot of privileges as well. Sometimes I'm sad about its being over but I'm that way about books and sunsets and conversations. The medicines I take don't grant my moods much independence, so I suspect these reactions, but I think they are my own. I have been a fool all my life, giving away large chunks of time and wasting years on nothing much. I had a mania for brave talk and some flirtation with or sense of possibility—and then I wanted to lie down and think about it. (Bernard Malamud once said that I had talked away a dozen books I might have written. I never told him how much time I spent lying down and staring at nothing.) And maybe I am being a fool now.

And I have died before, come close enough to dying

that doctors and nurses on those occasions said that those were death experiences, the approach to death, a little of death felt from the inside. And I have nursed dying people and been at deathbeds. I nearly died when my first mother did, leaving me practically an orphan at almost two years old. (My real father, Max Weintrub, was an illiterate local junk man, a semipro prizefighter in his youth and unhealably violent; I saw him off and on when I was growing up but never really knew him as a father. I was told that after my mother's death, he sold me to relatives—the Brodkeys—for three hundred dollars.) As an adult, at one point, I forced myself to remember what I could of the child's feelings. The feelings I have now are far milder. My work, my notions and theories and doctrines, my pride have conspired to make me feel as I do now that I am ill.

I have always remembered nearly dying when I was seven and had an allergic, hypothermic reaction coming out of anesthesia. When I was thirty, a hepatitis thing was misdiagnosed as cancer of the liver, and I was told I had six weeks to live. The sensations at those various times were not much alike, but the feeling of extreme sickness, of being racked, was and is the same, as is the sense of real death.

I have wondered at times if maybe my resistance to the fear-of-death wasn't laziness and low mental alertness, a cowardly inability to admit that horror was horror, that dying was unbearable. It feels, though, like a life-giving rebelliousness, a kind of blossoming. Not a love of death but maybe a love of God. I wouldn't want to be hanged and it would kill my soul to be a hangman but I always hoped that if I were hanged I would be amused and superior, and capable of having a good time somehow as I died—this may be a sense of human style in an orphan, greatly damaged and deadened, a mere sense of style overriding a more normal terror and sense of an injustice of destiny. Certainly, it is a *dangerous* trait. I am not sensible . . . At all times I am more afraid of anesthesia and surgery than I am of death. I have had moments of terror, of abject fear. I was rather glad to have those moments. But the strain was tremendous. My feelings of terror have had a scattered quality mostly, and I tended to despise them as petty. I have more fear of cowardice and of being broken by torture than I do of death. I am aware of my vulnerability, of how close I come to being shattered. But next to that is a considerable amount of nerve—my blood parents and real grandparents were said to have been insanely brave, to have had an arrogant sangfroid about their courage and what it allowed them to do. They had, each of them, a strong tropism toward the epic. My mother, before I was born, traveled alone from near Leningrad to Illinois in the 1920s, a journey that, at her social level, took nearly two months. The year before, her older brother had disappeared in transit, perhaps murdered. My father once boxed a dozen men in a row one evening on a bet and supposedly laid all the women under thirty who lined up afterward. Another time, better attested, with two other men he took on a squad of marching local Nazis in St. Louis, twenty-five or thirty men, and won.

One of the things that struck me when I was first told that I had AIDS was that I was cut off from my family inheritance of fatal diseases—the strokes and high blood pressure and cancer and tumors of my ancestors. My medical fate turned out to be quite different.

I felt a bit orphaned again, and idiosyncratic, but strangely also as if I had been invited, almost abducted, to a party, a somber feast but not entirely grim, a feast of the seriously afflicted who yet were at war with social indifference and prejudice and hatred. It seemed to me that I was surrounded by braveries without number, that I had been inducted into a phalanx of the wildly-alive-even-if-dying, and I felt honored that I would, so to speak, die in the company of such people.

What will happen to us? Is death other than silence and nothingness? In my grazing experiences of it, it is that disk of acceptance and of unthreading and disappearance at the bottom of the chute of revenant memories, ghosts and the living, the gauntlet of important recollections through which one is forced in order to approach the end of one's consciousness. Death itself is soft, softly lit, vastly dark. The self becomes taut with metamorphosis and seems to give off some light and to have a not-quite-great-enough fearlessness toward that immensity of the end of individuality, toward one's absorption into the dance of particles and inaudibility. Living, one undergoes one metamorphosis after another—often they are cockroach states, inset with moments of passivity with the sense of real death—but they are continuous and linked. This one is a stillness and represents a sifting out of identity and its stories, a breaking off or removal of the self, and a devolution into mere effect and memory, outspread and not tightly bound but scattered among micromotions and as if more windblown than in life. Or this is what I imagine, on the approach.

AIDS had never been one of our serious fears. It was not one of my secret dreads. I am so shaken by what has occurred that I tend to remember crazily or like someone tortured. I have lost much of the discipline of memory, yet I remember what should have seemed significant at the time. Ellen and I were in Berlin and then in Venice, meeting with publishers and translators, and some people—everyone, really—said I was too thin. Ellen began to worry when a blackish, caved-in spot appeared in my right cheek, but I thought it was the macrobiotic diet I was trying to follow. The poetry of being recognized and accepted as an important writer in Berlin and then in Venice while I was sickening in some way I could not understand presents to me a dark beauty of complete wreckage. I think, too, that when I heard the news from Barry there was already in part of my mind some literary sense of death, of suicide, as the appropriate outcome. I had written a novel in one year, a novel I liked, that I was proud of; I had expected the effort to kill me. I was subject to strange exhaustions and was wobbly on airplanes, but beyond that I was strained past my level of strength by the difference in reputation and treatment I received in various countries—great artist here, fool there, major writer, minor fake, villain, virtuoso, jerk, hero.

Life is a kind of horror. It is OK, but it is wearing. Enemies and thieves don't lay off as you weaken. The wicked flourish by being ruthless even then. If you are ill, you have to have a good lawyer. When you are handed a death sentence, the newly redrawn battle lines are enclosed. Depending on your circumstances, in some cases you have to back off and lie low. You're weak. Death feels preferable to daily retreat.

Certainly people on the street who smile gently at me as I walk slowly or X-ray attendants calling me *darling* or *lovey* are aware of this last thing. A woman I know who died a few years back spoke of the inescapable sympathy for weakness. She hated it. I don't want to talk about my dying to everyone, or over and over. Is my attitude only vanity—and more vanity—in the end? In a sense, I steal each day, but I steal it by making no effort. It is just there, sunlight or rain, nightfall or morning. I am still living at least a kind of life, and I don't want to be reduced to an image now, or, in my own mind, feel I am spending all my time on my dying instead of on living, to some satisfying extent, the time I have left.

If you train yourself as a writer to look at these things—this vulnerability, when the balance is gone and the defenses are undone so that you are open to viruses and their shocking haywire excitement—then facing them becomes almost habitual. You will have the real material, and it will arise from this new-to-you, dense memory of being jostled by medical and natural violence to the edge of life.

People like to speak of *what really happened....* The New York *agreement* among people of my sort is that everything about one another's lives is knowable. You take a few clues, regard them with sophistication, and you know *everything*. In the end, this is a city that acknowledges no mysteries, one that is set on prying, or getting, or revealing. I find New York talk horrendous, the personal conclusions stupid, the idealization of others' experience and the demonization of others' experience hateful and contemptible. And the bottom-lining, the judgments made as if all were known, the lies, the fraud, the infinite oral thuggery here of Jews and Gentiles alike, the cold ambition is, I repeat, unlivable.

What we really have in this city are able people, competent people, who as they rise in the world have more and more complicated professional lives. Quite logically, that eats them up, and the monstrous residue that is left is beyond emotion, but with an appetite for it, and a terrible and terrified longing and unsuitability for it. This monstrous residue is beyond friendship, beyond anything. (It *is* capable of truly marvelous, if ogreish, companionship.)

I have been lectured on this subject, told I am wrong

when I say what dregs they are, what dregs we are, what
a creeping madness our adulthood becomes. The above
has been denied to me by nearly everyone in New York.
But surely they must know.

I have no shyness now.

I can without hysterics describe the anal diddling
that probably led to the transmission of this virus and to
my death: I did go to bed with men, nameless, not
famous, men, who could not ask me for anything or
blame me for anything or expect revelation from me. I
could offer a list of the men I have had (or the women I
have had). But the real truth is that in this country sex is
not yet regarded as a fact of life.

The arts in the twentieth century have not pictured
the reality of actual sex and actual love as they are in
life, on actual days, over actual time, but instead have
tended to recoin them as, oh, socialist bliss, or as paradise before the nightmare strikes, or as nonexistent
(Joyce and Beckett, the sexual yet sexless Irishmen), or
as obsession and victimization (Freud and Proust), or as
some idyll of heat and whatnot. For me, the greatest
portrayer of high-art sexlessness was Balanchine,
because he captured and beautified so physically the
rage and longing and the attempts to escape loneliness.
And then there is Eliot; one should remember that
Lawrence was driven out of England while dry, sexless

Eliot came to be idolized. And perhaps rightly. Sex, after all, is unwise: look at me. The foolish nature of sexual love is there in front of you, always. Civic duty, ambition, even personal freedom are opposed to it. One appreciates the urge to sanitize and control, the punitive framework and the denial of sexual authenticity. (Think of Jon Vickers's singing, for instance. He caused embarrassment in American audiences as Sinatra never did. He caused embarrassment in the way Billie Holiday did— people sometimes called her impact *sinister*.)

But what happens in a competitive city, among people who are clever imitators, students, really (more or less sedulous apes), is that the paucity of such authenticity leads to the constant manufacture of what you might call a sore-nerved and sensitive counterfeit sex. Counterfeit sex is a large part of what New York is. People here rebel by means of a jealous promiscuity, a jealously restless sense of the possible happiness of others. What we have and live with is the institutionalization of sexual terror and sexual envy.

As for me, I will say peevishly that I was never accepted as gay by anyone, including someone who lived with me and claimed to be a lover. I did think that, for me, no decent relations were possible with women back then; the women were rotten with their self-expectation, their notions of femininity, their guilt. And I saw no male role I could play that was acceptable to me. Toward the end of my experience of homosexuality, before I met Ellen, I underwent the most outrageous banishment to a role of sheer, domineering, hated and worshipped masculinity.

I was never handsome. But until I was fifty, I almost never wore clothes in private. My nakedness had all sorts of meanings, including those of a goodish body for a vain man with insufficient money to buy good clothes. And a body to counterweigh the lost head. I stopped being interested in my body five years or so ago when I published *Stories in an Almost Classical Mode*—it was as neat as that. Now I have the strangest imaginable tie to my own flesh; my body to me is like a crippled rabbit that I don't want to pet, that I forget to feed on time, that I haven't time to play with and get to know, a useless rabbit kept in a cage that it would be cruel to turn loose. It doesn't have a prayer for survival. Or any chance of an easy death. It is mere half-eaten prey. Like a captured snake or rabbit in an Audubon.

But I know people, crippled and uncrippled, who have felt that way all their lives. So I am not complaining now. I am even a bit amused at the irony that I might complain. I am only saying that I am prejudiced toward a nakedness in print—toward embodiment in black-and-white.

Not constantly but not inconstantly either, underneath the sentimentality and obstinacy of my attitudes,
are, as you might expect, a quite severe rage and a vast,
a truly extensive terror, anchored in contempt for you
and for life and for everything. I believe that the world is
dying, not just me. And fantasy will save no one. The
deathly unreality of Utopia, the merchandizing of
Utopia is wicked, *deadly* really.

Now Ellen and I traded places on physical strength. I
wanted to be a good sport about it. In what I once called
our regular life, because of the disparity in our sizes (she
is nearly a foot shorter and weighs at least sixty pounds
less), we had been physically close in a defiant way
encoded with all sorts of mutual mockeries and defenses
against each other—all of which were still present, in
ghostly irony, in pallid nostalgia. The sensitive and
tactful nursing she did included a startling respect for
what was *left* of my strength. (This re-created me at
moments, as when I woke from a nap in pain.) She
wasn't tearful about its disappearance. She watched it
ebb with tenderness. To be honest, it kept as a presence
in the raw air a quasi-sexual intimacy.

I understood it but not entirely. The pattern was just
the two of us in a room, with her, in her usual defiance of

ordinariness, performing a honeymoon-of-death obser-
vance with a kind of gravity, a bit like a Japanese cere-
monial occasion. Extinction was just a piece of shit off to
one side: who gave a shit about death? Everything that
mattered was in the pride and utter seriousness of the
ceremony. It was a kind of snobbery toward death.

An American male idiom is *this fucking intimacy*. (The
phrase can, as you know, imply a kind of impatience with
intimacy as well as the sexual nature of it, depending on
your voice and on whether you smile when you say it.) In
Ellen, who reconstituted me, this was expressed as a
kind of merciful echo of my moods. She was hostess in
the narrow hospital room to my mothers, my mothers'
ghosts or spirits, and to the line of fathers, the four mil-
lennia of unkillable Jewish males in their conceited stiff-
neckedness, then to all the dead and dying literary
figures, then to all the characters who die in the books I
most admire (I can't bear death scenes in movies)—
Prince Andrei and Hadji Murad and Proust's narrator's
grandmother—and then to all the widowed women back
to Andromache or Hecuba. And she made room for the
nurses and the nurses' aides, for the interns and the
residents, for Barry. I have never seen such intent or
such subtle seduction: I cannot even begin to describe
the silent promises, the hidden blessings she promised
them, she promised them all, the ghosts, too. And

Death, standing over me and stirring up the muck that refused to be the bottom in the onslaught of the revolting pneumonia.

I lived through Ellen's will from time to time during those days. I had her agility and subtlety vicariously. I had that merciful depth of her female self at my disposal. It was like that as long as she was awake, anyway, and as long as her strength held out. At the same time I felt a bit cheated, while she was awake, of the mortal solitude that I expected to meet with at what I took to be the end.

Our regular lives, our once-usual life together, had been reproduced in a truncated form in a hospital room: flowers, fruit, a newspaper, quibbling with each other, a certain seclusion, a habit of judging—the usual things, even at death's door, in death's presence.

But it was a hospital room, and I was dying, and I didn't have many private emotions. The husband in this marital scene was drugged to the teeth with prednisone, a steroid that walls off physical pain and depression by creating a strange pre-craziness of its own. I felt a rather awful clarity of humor, a nauseated comic sense; I was in an odd state. And the wife in the scene was overly gentle, sickroom gentle, terrified and obstinately hopeful—not her usual self. She was afraid of gloom in this well-intentioned parody-caricature of our former life. The

moments of grief I had were immediately contagious—
well, the room was very small.

We would hold hands and I would say, "Oh shit" or
"This *is* shitty," and we would cry a bit. It seemed like a
sufficient amount of poetry. I would say, "Well, who
cares?" or "I don't like this mushy stuff. Let's stop."

Equally invasive were the tender moments, Ellen
bathing me and turning me, ninety-seven-pound Ellen,
or changing the bed. Or helping me into the bathroom. I
had to be propped on her and on the wheeled pole of the
IV. I was determined to spare her my excrement. My
head lolled. My legs gave way.

I had no strength, but it is true that willpower can do
a great deal. It can't halt or cure AIDS, but it can mock
death and weakness: it can mock these things sometimes. Our bedtime talk or our toilet talk had to avoid
sentiment; I had no strength for sentiment. I showed off
for Ellen. I talked about business and money, about the
information I'd negotiated from the doctor.

But she was the one with hope. She was the one with
the sense of drama. She was the one who, with some, ah,
degree of untruth, exclaimed on being told that she was
HIV-negative, "Oh, I don't want to be clear. I want to
have it, too."

An emotional remark. A bit of a marital lie, of marital manipulation. But true enough in that if I decided to

kill myself she was still determined, so she said, to kill herself, too.

She wanted to die of what I was going to die of.

"That's bullshit, honey. It isn't what I want. Just can it, OK?"

I am peculiarly suited to catastrophe because of my notions and beliefs; I am accustomed to reconstituting myself in the middle of catastrophe. And my ideas, my language, support me in the face of disastrous horror over and over. I am like a cockroach, perhaps—with vanity, now with AIDS, with a cowardice much greater than that of Kafka's Samsa.

Ellen is not like that. She has an identity, of the real, familied sort. (She has written two novels, both of which illustrate this.) A good many people, including me, care about her. Her children are never alone in the world, and that sometimes irks them. She was once rich and is at times so grateful to have her own feelings without reference to money that she can seem happy in the manner of an escaped convict. She is gullible toward bad news in a rebelliously saintly way that tends to irritate me. Her rebelliousness extends throughout her existence—it is toward God and death, toward society, toward men. How she reconciles that with the propriety she manifests day in and day out is beyond me. So little has been written (or at least published) by women who feel as she does

that she has had to be, as a woman, her own prophet.
Her code is unworded. You can categorize her emotion
quite easily but you cannot define it. You cannot ever
demand it. Or even trick her into it. She will let some
people trick her, but she has a bored, brittle quality
then. I tell her we are cowards and artists and are in
flight and are and have to be awful people to get our
work done. She ignores me when I talk this way. She
does and does not believe what I say or what I believe. "I
cannot live like that," is what she says. I mean, I can see,
often, the degree of *enlistment* in her being with me.

I have a number of kinds of humility, but I am arrogant. I am semi-famous, and I see what I see. I examine
everything that is put in front of me, like a jeweler. I
am a Jew from the Midwest, not at all like a New York
Jew. I am so arrogant that I believe a formulation only if
it has the smell or lift of inspiration. I have never, since
childhood, really expected to be comforted.

I inherit from my blood father and my blood mother and
her father considerable physical strength. One time, as
I said earlier, when I was seven, I nearly died, because
of an allergic reaction to an anesthetic, the ether deri-
vatives then in use. (My real mother returned in a hal-
lucination, and I found it unbearable.) I went into

convulsions and, according to the machines and measurements, I died: my heart stopped, my breathing stopped. Some young doctors and nurses and one old nurse saved me. I can remember their bustling labor, even the nervous smell coming off them. I had been more or less legitimately dead, but I managed to get up and walk partway across the hospital room that evening. My adoptive father called me Rasputin for a while: "Nothing can kill you."

Sick or well, all my life I've had enough strength for whatever I set out to do. But this time, no. That degree of strength was over. Now I knew how my parents felt when their strength failed. It is extremely irritating. Certain melodramatic speeches do come to mind: "Kill me and get it over with." They both said that. I said it once or twice myself, but with more irony. I would save my strength and then leap—biliously, worm-in-the-muddishly—into speech: "This goddamn hospital bed is so uncomfortable you might as well *kill me and get it over with.*"

I was always aware mentally of the rather awful certainty of death, of the physical, sensory fact, but only in words. I mean the mind looked on, weakly, and saw the situation as a folkish joke, like a newspaper headline: THREAT OF DEATH FOR HAROLD, or HAROLD IS GOING TO GET IT THIS TIME, or H. R. BRODKEY

FINDS WHAT IT'S LIKE TO SUCK MUD. With a
subheadline: THIS IS ROTTEN, SAYS EX-AMATEUR ATH-
LETE. And then the subheads: "The Statistics Look *Bad*,"
and "Killer-Diller Pneumonia Strikes 'New Yorker'
Writer."

My adoptive parents were ill for most of my childhood, and I was aware of the implacable dissimilarity
between the people and events in the active world and
the people and events in the grip of medical reality, the
medicines scouring and wrecking, or surgical interven-
tion doing that, or radiation. My adoptive father, Joe
Brodkey, had raged and grieved. My blood father, Max,
had suffocated—he had something that was described to
me as senile asthma: the asthma starved his heart, and
his heart gave out. And he had raged and cursed, as did
my adoptive mother, Doris, who had cancer and told all
those around her that *they were getting on her nerves*. I was
prepared for the irritability or even madness of being a
patient, but except for the suffocation, none of those
things was happening to me. I felt very little of anything,
I mean as comment. It was a relief to have the illness
unmasked, to have Death be openly present. It was a
relief to get away from the tease and rank of imputed
greatness and from the denial and attacks and from my
own sense of things, of worldly reality and of literary
reality—all of it. In the last few years, mental and phy-

sical revulsion toward the literary empire-builders and the masters of fakery had grown to the point where hiding and containing it had been a bit like having tumors that cleared up whenever I was upstate in the wilds or in Europe. The inadequacies of the work these people did and in the awful work they fostered, the alternate revulsion and pity they aroused, I had had enough of. It was truly a perceptible relief to be out of their reach and into another sort of experience, even if it was terminal.

It was a relief to have the future not be my speculative responsibility anymore and to escape from games of superiority and inferiority.

Yet I couldn't sleep; I was able on the prednisone only to doze in a kind of shallow unconsciousness, and perhaps in fear, I dozed better by day than at night. I believe in sleep. In the past, when I was ill, or even just sad, I would sleep it off.

When Ellen slept, I expected to meet, as it were, my own grief and mortal loneliness. When I dozed, I expected phantoms and nightmares. It was not like that. I woke each time precariously placed in horizontal stillness, protecting my heart and lungs as I had with my posture when I was awake. I woke aware that I'd dreamed, and there was a fraction's hesitation before it became obvious I would not remember my dreams, that they had been about death and that my waking self would not reproduce any part of them for me. But I knew they had been gentle. I woke without the slightest confusion; in my weakness I knew who I was and where I was and what my predicament was. I did not once imagine myself well—or safe. I woke in a secondary mental chamber, as if I were an Olympic runner of illness and death, one who would lose this time but who had trained off and on throughout his life for this. And so I woke prepared to play the day's game again.

God as a term for all of whatever reality there is— the universe, all the universes—God as a term used by my soul seems to signal that *He* loves the present tense even more than consciousness does. (I tend to refer to God as He, but I do it without thinking of him as male particularly.) Our sense of presentness usually proceeds in waves, with our minds tumbling off into wandering. Usually, we return and ride the wave and tumble and resume the ride and tumble, and in the act of tumbling we are ourselves, egocentrically, and things are seen and known to us. *Actual reality may belong to the present tense, but this falling away and return is what we are.* But I was too tired for that; no argument, not even full mathematical logic, could short-circuit or alter the dominant nature of the present tense. This time, in these moments, I had nowhere to tumble to. It was all present tense.

Medical attention and the horrors of death, great death, amused me in a quiet way. Amused? Well, what do you feel when you're expected to fight an often-fatal pneumonia and you've been sentenced to death already? You are death meat. I don't see how you can cooperate in any ordinary way. You are a foot soldier, cannon fodder. Various functions of the body are endangered routinely. Tediously, you endure. You live in the tidal influx and efflux of medication. You make an attempt to go on as a person in the world. You smile at Barry. You smile at Ellen. You lie very still. But there is the grotesquerie of the patient, the mad person, the electrical flesh. The connection to the ordinary world is broken, yet not entirely. And there is a cartoon aspect: the curses people hurled at you have come true. What do you suggest I do? Be unamused?

And Barry meant to amuse, in the sense that he meant to give me a jolt, a blast of energy and momentum. It was as if he caromed in and set us, like billiard balls, bounding about the narrow room mentally, with animation. At times, he was exhausted and maybe depressed, but he hid it almost rapturously, with medical-businesslike adjustments, with watchfulness. He worked in relation to a not yet fully understood disease using clinical experience and analogy. Really, I was grateful that he bothered. His respect for my life verged on the idiotic. He could not win. Literally, he shone and prescribed and analyzed and stole for me a month here, perhaps two years there. He kept studying medications and my face and my eyes while he was handling other patients, studying other faces and other eyes. Barry was moving fast inside a straight line, a medical frame, without much respect for the inevitable medical defeat. He put on a show, put up a fight, and I applauded as best I could. The spirit was cracked in me, but I offered what version of spirit I could to him. I joined the coarseness of struggle: this was my loyalty to the regular world.

I ride for a while on my limited breath, on the cadence, the meter of it, in obedience to the muse of immediate survival. I am still unable to breathe without oxygen and am racked by my reactions to the huge amounts of medication dripping or pumping into me, or swallowed—a handful of pills at what is euphemistically referred to as bedtime.

Barry says, "You're fine . . . You have to be careful . . . We're monitoring your potassium . . ." *You're not sink-*

ing . . . You won't be sent to the ICU today . . . With some luck
we'll make it . . . You can have another fragment of life.

I am inside an experience that the doctor cannot
share from the inside, yet the reports he gives me and
the actions he takes at a given moment are the only real
source of news I have about myself. AIDS is a famous
disease that is simultaneously of little day-to-day import.
I wrote down *Barry insisted that I be clear in my mind what*
having AIDS means. Actually, at his urging, I spoke up and
named it myself. But I knew very little about it. What I
think he wanted me to know is that AIDS is the ter-
minus in a thus far fatal viral infestation, which was
identified in 1981–82 and arbitrarily, perhaps not finally
usefully, defined to conform to surface symptomology.
Roughly, this means that when you have AIDS, you're
hospital material. The terminology is distinctive: you
will die of "complications from AIDS." Babes and old
geezers are special prey to the stubborn murderer *Pneu-*
mocystis. Whoever you are, your biological identity now
occupies a thin cage with prowling, opportunistic diseases. AIDS is not phallocentric, not homocentric, not
picky in the least about its carrion; it is in the service of
the grandeur of opportunism.

"You won't be bothered by interns," Barry said. They
do not flock to your room, nor do doctors meet to discuss

what is killing you. This is pragmatism, not prejudice. You are a lousy conversation piece.

The separation from society, the political marginalization and the financial thefts, the attacks to see what can be stolen from you, and the indignity—including social indignity—of AIDS suggest a partial, sometimes fluorescent and linoleumed version of the death camps. Those who postpone the final crescendoing of the humiliations—wasting, dementia, diarrhea, thrush, PML (which affects the brain), Kaposi's Sarcoma, certain exotic glaucomas—for more than a year or two are sometimes called *survivors*, in what seems a recognition of cousinship.

The aura of punishment is simply present: a *Walpurgisnacht*. For those who survive awhile, the fall lies in wait. You are caught in the camp just below the surface of your seeming freedom. You stare through the wire. The illness leaves very little room for courage and yet it seems to ignite a maddened courage in many. Then, too, some sufferers, as a result of their previous and varied refusals to submit, already have a curious pact with shamelessness, a quality of banditry. Some homosexuals have it, some hemophiliacs have it, too.

I made these observations along the spine of a more systematic one: hospitals have become a mess; they've lost it. The breakdown of the middle-class conspiracy that was urban culture in the West shows in hospitals as a visible and basic and entire decay. Everything is improvisatory and shaky, even cleanliness and the administration of treatment. But perhaps because of obstinate kindness in some people, a determination to embody goodness, or some addiction to the priority of emergency, or because the meaning of rescuing someone from death appeals to the soul or to their sense of importance in the universe, the best nurses and nurse's aides appear and take care of you when you are dying.

Or, I should say, I got that kind of care. I got more of it if Ellen was there. The medicine came on time, the IV was properly adjusted—and the attention, in its smallest details, had in it an element of respectful shoving at the body and the spirit in its fall, a funny kind of summoning, an American summoning, not to glory but to make use of the technology and techniques of treatment, to profit from them. One is expected to make an effort to return to suburbia, to the tennis court, to make an obeisance to life.

I had already browbeaten Barry into saying that there are no miracles, no cures here. No one has been rescued from AIDS so far. AIDS statistics are not beautiful. Life expectancies in 1981 of eleven months from the onset of full-blown AIDS have since been raised, statistically, by 1993, to eighteen months. A great many people don't make it that far. And much of that advance represents the six months AZT seems to confer by stirring up the bone marrow and giving you a new influx of T-cells, or white cells.

The practical limit of survival varies, but one hears a lot about two to five years. Someone with a strong constitution, a middle-class protectionist sort of medical history and middle-class nourishment is more likely to make it to eighteen months. Once you get that far, you then have a better chance at three years. After that it's very iffy again. The second round of brute winnowing begins. The very fortunate might last another year. To last five years is a triumph.

As a prize, as a goal, it is not very *American*. It is not Utopian, although Barry tried to make it that way with amazing generosity; he would raise his voice and smile, and I would see the changing brilliance of light in his eyes; he would look like an inspired pitchman, and he would produce his pitch for *life*. But it's not life.

Optimism. Hopefulness. Our American fondness for the ad pitch and our dependence on it culturally to represent not what works or is worth preserving but what is worth our working *for*—this, in lieu of tradition, is nervously life-giving. It is also a madness of sorts, a dream-taunted avidity for the future to replace a sense of history. But it is the basis of America—the forward-looking thing. We-will-create-a-nation, and we will have gardens and swimming pools and corrective surgery. Franklin Roosevelt's speeches—if you compare them with Churchill's, you can see what I'm talking about. You can see it in the rhythms and in the imagery and in the statements. Roosevelt proposed the four freedoms, and Churchill offered blood, toil, sweat, and tears. (Or compare Twain with Wodehouse. Or Groucho Marx with Waugh.) The American sense of tragedy is so diluted by daydream as to seem almost ridiculous. We Americans create symbols helter-skelter, as a form of advertising, an active unreality. Compare Churchill's cigar with Roosevelt's cigarette holder. (Or Churchill's drinking, which was overt, with Roosevelt's wheelchair, which was virtually never photographed.) The Declaration of Independence and the Constitution and the Bill of Rights are strangely like ad texts, guarantees of the sort that you find in ads. And advertising is to nihilism and threats of heaven and hell as matter is to anti-matter. The foundations of middle-classness in America have nothing to do with social class in the European sense and everything to do with a Utopian attempt.

The American equivalent (which is hardly equivalent) of the landed gentry is a socially wobbly market of consumers who are rich and arrogant as all get-out, easily intimidated yet not easily restrained. Here, because the culture is so unsteady (and so new), it is the how-to element that dominates—how to be *happy* or reasonably comfortable and in comfortable circumstances; how to deal with superior sorts of people who have status, who, say, enjoy opera; how to do these things in the near, improved future. The inflection has a "Which side are you on?" quality to it. The American daydream, as in Twain (and Hemingway), is about rebuilding after the flood, about being better off than before, about outwitting this or that challenge, up to and including death.

Well, how do you manage to be optimistic *for the moment*? Without hope?

No one can explain what it means to be marked out. The usual explanations, the traditional ones, have to do with sin—sins of the fathers and your own sins. But to be American is to be Nietzschean in half of yourself. You move beyond sin even if part of you still believes in it. You—or anyone—have to suffer your life and death under civil law, so to speak.

Part of the self is made of one's work; you get glimpses of meaning in that. A sense of your crimes can perhaps help keep you alive. Or self-righteous indignation can save you. And a refusal to fight becomes a method of fighting, of gruffly asserting control, as in *Look, I don't know how long I can live like this.* Then the doors fly open as in a farce, and something like Medusa's head swings into the corridors of illness like the end of a pendulum, turning you to stone.

I kept wanting to cry out, as Doris Brodkey had, or take refuge in rage, as Joe Brodkey had. I wanted an inherited death. But I had, indeed, lost the past. This death seemed entirely mine, mine and Ellen's alone.

Death is not soft-mouthed, vague-footed, nearby. It is in the hall. The weakness does not wash over me and disappear but stays. It has a stagnant air. It floods me, and the flood is soul-wide. The casing that my youth and strength and luck came in is empty and vibrates a bit. A fox cub, a small bird nervous in the shadow, a bag of tainted blood, a skeletal and stiff figure lying still is what my consciousness is. And it is like a small bird's being fed to have one's whispered wishes taken seriously and to be spared predatory sympathy. Barry and Ellen are going to save me for a while.

I am only flittingly in the present in my hospital room. I
am at moments wide open to the world again, enveloped
by life in a small Midwestern town called Alton where I
was taken by my adoptive parents. My new mother was a
Daisy Buchanan type, though Jewish. One time when
she had me with her and couldn't find a parking spot,
she left her car in the middle of the street, blocking the
trolley line, and told a traffic cop to take care of it, which
he did. Style in Alton was overtly determined by money
and access to St. Louis, which was across the river. Each
large city had something like an empire of small towns it
ruled; it took two days and a night on a train to get from
St. Louis to New York. The local storekeepers and the
police knew you. (This led to a terrific amount of sexual
freedom if you were "respectable.") The Sears, Roebuck
and the Montgomery Ward were your national retailers.
Most of the roads had been laid out for horse and buggy,
and some took right-angle turns to follow property
lines. Some country roads were made of brick. I always
thought that the yellow brick road in *The Wizard of Oz*
was a rain-wet brick road between cornfields, reflecting
sunshine.

Alton had thirty thousand inhabitants who experimented variously with the oxymoron of "American style"

in that period, the rich wearing St. Louis clothes and the richer wearing St. Louis's version of New York clothes or even Paris clothes and hats and gloves. In those years the great difference between small-town style and big-city style was that the latter was aimed at the future, at something to come. It suggested romance and a further step into cosmopolitan legend, into the next episode of a story about power. Small-town style, as would later be true of suburban style, was not forward-looking; it was, just about absolutely, anti-future, which is to say anti-story, frozen, codified, idyllic. So that even if a woman got her hands on a Schiaparelli or a Mainbocher, it was a set piece, a sort of bossy, final outfit. This was because real style—the visual casting of yourself in the daring light of what you might wish for or be capable of doing—would, in the course of things, take you right out of town and into adventure, and very few had that much nerve.

My parents had not a great deal of money but enough nerve to move to St. Louis, in 1934; there we had no connections, we were not stylish. Even a child as young as I could feel the difference. Joe Brodkey, my adoptive father, used to go back to Alton once a week just to sniff at the memories of the time when we had been influential and had had *position*. My family had mattered in a small town, but they did not matter in St. Louis. Joe Brodkey had that sense of American toughness which

is so discouraging in someone who has almost nothing of
what he really wants.

Do you know the myth of my *irresistibility*? It isn't easy to
talk about. The Fuck You Dreamed Of, Maybe. What a
joke. It was a matter of rumor—of reputation, all part of
the floating aura, the sharp aroma of New York gossip. I
practiced amateurishly and assiduously, and with some
enjoyment and curiosity, but I wasn't up to it. My sexual
limits were physically very clear. I failed to be a hero of
the 1960s. Or of the 1970s. I wasn't up to the role. I was
odd, demanding, and evasive. I never approached styl-
ishness and acts that Mapplethorpe pictured and made
public. I was never in the Casanova range. What I did
and whatever actual events fueled the image—whatever
humor or vanity I showed—it was clear that most of the
myth was based on the claims and gossip of others. I had
a life, but not that one.

   Tennessee Williams, who went to my high school
long before I got there, and who had some of the same
teachers, touched on the subject of male irresistibility
in terms of hustlers and handsome strangers passing
through town, always in rags, and subject to humiliation. In imitation, William Inge dealt with it more
directly, more reportorially, in the play (later the movie)

Picnic. And such actors as Paul Newman, Marlon Brando, and William Holden for a while embodied this notion in various roles in Hollywood, getting shot and falling into the swimming pool and so on.

The American representation of The Good Fuck (an experience you owe yourself) always dealt with the childishness of such figures and with their failure in the world—handsome orphans, beaten down, beaten back, dependent on aging movie stars or on Anna Magnani as a moneyed storekeeper in a small town or on Kim Novak's depth as a woman; these sexy, bankrupt, Christlike orphans, these phallus bearers and suppliers were by definition without power in the world. Brando had trouble playing Napoleon or Marc Antony or any other type but the phallic martyr. And the highly successful writers, the troubled Williams especially, and the successful and power-mad directors could never suppress their contempt for these men in their degrees of failure and lack of power. Billy Wilder's version in *Sunset Boulevard* is the most contemptuous. I don't know of any British versions of such male irresistibility in the writing of the modern era, except for Basil Seal in Waugh's books, and he is a killer at heart. Lermontov and Stendhal and Pushkin are kinder but still cruel. Some of the more ancient versions, such as Joseph or David in the Bible, are treated with less contempt, but then they are pictured in their worldly power, their success; they are said to be blessed. The American version is always a fool.

It seems hardly earthshaking, this crap of irresistibility, but in life, in the literal reality this takes, it means gasps and anger at you and people crying because of you and a lot of gossip and various abduction attempts and threats of suicide because of you and your being followed on the street by people who are obsessed with you seriously, ludicrously. It means people hating you for a betrayal that never occurred, for what they feel is your luck, which they then want in their rage to undo. It is fantastically embarrassing to say that I was adopted illegally and with great difficulty, and the difficulty was accepted because of the infant's, the very young child's—the tales agree even if the photographs don't—extreme beauty. The supposed beauty of a catatonic toddler as a small-town public "myth" among Jews is the substance of childhood drama—this irresistibility, these looks, these bones and features. From infancy, my life has always been, always, always, on the verge of my being eaten alive: *I could just eat you up.* In my childhood, people talked a great deal about me and quarreled over me—and threatened force. And there was violence, some of it directed at me.

I have seen, as an adult, children of such attention

become quite violent themselves, and hysterical, and strange. I think of childhood and adolescence as sexual, as filled with the sexual intrusion of others. I was told that Doris Brodkey first tried to buy me from my real mother when I was a year old. I would suspect that the fate of irresistibility in the ordinary world is established in infancy as a condition of existence for most of us. But that in my case has also partly determined my death.

I remember people coming to the house to see me—I remember being brought out after being dressed and combed, and being passed from embrace to embrace. I had a sand-colored cashmere short-pants suit with a Little Lord Fauntleroy frill at the neck and down the front, which made it impossible for me to button. My parents and my sister and my nurse used to take turns doing the buttons and brushing my ringletted blond hair curl by curl. How I hated to be touched. Or even looked at. Sometimes I would kick and scream and not allow my nurse to dress me. I would even climb out the window of my second-floor room and hide on the roof rather than go downstairs. I loved dirt and anything resembling boots. I wanted to wear galoshes every day.

It was commonly said, "That child needs discipline." You'd be surprised how odd—and troubling—a child's "No" was back in the 1930s, and how temperamentally the grownups reacted. Decades later, in New York, in almost any field of endeavor, when a sexual proposition was made to you by anyone, for you to say "No" seemed to mark you as an amateur, as unprofessional, unserious, and to some extent as a fool. But I was so proud, so possessed by ghosts, that even when I made up my mind to say "Yes"—to this person or that person, to an offer of shelter, say—what came out of my mouth was "No."

Really, one sees people cursed with irresistibility as being finally interesting for how they fail. For how they can be hurt. For how they retreat, become scarred, or obese, or dead. When I am attacked, it reminds me of my childhood. Spite and the desire to humble you combine uncertainly in an angry way to make you laugh with shock and secret recognition. Sanity becomes very pronounced in you, as a defense. Every touch verges on abuse, on recruitment.

Few people will ever see you without an affronted sense of their own irresistibility and of themselves as objects of competing emotion. This trait makes others feel that you are taking something large and valuable away from them, and if you believe we know things by comparison or if you believe in democratic (competitive) exhibitionism, then you *are* taking something of value away from them: their projection of themselves as more worth loving than you are.

I was *in fashion* in New York in terms of this irresistibility off and on for the last forty years. And it was an insiderish thing to be "in love" with me at those times. Other people won literary prizes or academic honors. *I* discriminated among emotions and suitors—and judged their quality as people, their odors, their intelligence, their powers of comedy and of being thrilling, their emotional intelligence. I had always, explosively, a kind of emotional citizenship, an undeserved welcome. I felt this absurd irresistibility as a form of comedy. I am trying to describe the nature of the temptation offered to the child and by the child, then the adolescent, then the young man in New York who is now the aging man with AIDS.

Another man might "love" me like someone cheating at croquet, but the croquet court laid out in *me*, a pleasure ground of a peculiar sort. You play dumb and pretend to be respectable, but you are an old, old hand, an aged whore at this stuff. Outwardly, you perhaps are more distinguished and puritan in your air than that. No one need admit that you are this sort of person. People who become obsessed with you like to tell you that you're nothing special, that you're ugly—a certain amount of high and low melodrama lies in wait for you every day. Ah, the bitter phone calls. I cannot find in memory a day in my life without some erotic drama or other. And the temper with which you bear your history—the erotic slyness or directness—may give you a quality very like beauty, whatever your history is, whatever you actually look like. Perhaps it is a real beauty, the courage to have had a life of some sort, in spite of the difficulty, I mean.

Anyway, the major drama of my adolescence was that my adoptive father, Joe Brodkey, who was ill with heart trouble (a handsome invalid, as one would write in pornography) assailed me every day for two years, sexually—twice a day, every morning and every evening, when I was twelve and thirteen. He had nothing else to do, really. He was ill. We were not the same blood. I am being very shy. He never succeeded in entering me, but it was somewhat scary and sweaty. Except that there was the pathos of his dying. And there was my long history of boring irresistibility. And my mind, which was watching all of it. His blood pressure was fragilely high. I was too strong, too frozen, for very much to happen, for the drama to develop.

I am lying. I had to notice that he was heartsick—with feeling, clearly in *love*, in a way. And soon, somehow, when I didn't make a scene about the assaults, or whatever, a great many people knew about "the love story." I suppose my mother talked about it for reasons of her own. My mother said he-can't-live-without-you things and he's-hooked-you-have-him-where-you-want-him-you-talk-to-him-for-me things. Or Dad talked about it— he had rather nineteenth-century ideas of family and male rights.

I confessed nothing. I complained to no one. My mother, herself ill with cancer and drugged, warned me oracularly, "If I were you, I'd learn to keep my mouth shut." I don't mean to be insulting to her memory, but she was excited, even inspired, by the situation, which— it took no great brains to see—helped keep both her and Dad alive: it interested them, this *love* thing.

Such assaults as Joe's have their aspect of wanting to lower you, but at moments everything was focused, as if in the last line of a story, on a profound concern having to do with the creature in whom my identity was at the moment caught. Either of my parents would have killed the other for me. Sometimes they fought over me, and it seemed to be to the death—this is not uncommon, is it? My mother said advisingly, "You never seem nice if you have to say no." I was a "fine-looking young fella" (which I never actually quite was; I was weirder than that), "a young man with a good smile, if you want my opinion." She said, "You make do with what you're given." It was what she had to play with, what she had to move on the suburban board, in the terminal boredom of her life.

Still, for me, there was the drama, the persecution.

And such assaults, such oddities, comic and manic or melancholy or dangerous, occurred everywhere, as if by contagion—with the football guys, with old friends, with the mothers of friends, with strangers. I was even half-abducted once, forced into a car, but I fought and talked my way out of it. At school, my God, girls waited for me in the hall, or in front in good weather. Twice in one year, four times all in all, the mothers of girls whose approaches to me I had ignored complained to the school principal that I had hurt their daughters' feelings, and couldn't I be made to respond? My parents were telephoned, were talked to. Whatever I was, it was not taken to be a private property and mine. I understood my father's actions on this level, in this light.

One of the troubles with the reality of the passage of time is that the past can be lied about. False precedent can be argued. Unexamined realities can be dropped from conscious equations. The thing itself, the sexualized courtship, arose from the boy's comforting and, on occasion, holding and rocking his forty-four-year-old father when his father was racked by death-fever or rage or panic. Life perhaps was defined by one's code of behavior. I would start to laugh and accept an embrace briefly, then cut it short. It is your own moral judgment that arranges this refusal of your father even though he is dying. Such refusal is arrogant toward Daddy. Or at least it places a positive value on your own life. To ignore the feelings you arouse is indistinguishable from narcissism to someone who wants your attention. I am not complaining. I noticed that the denial of truth was what everyone called *tact*. He accursed me. Now I will die disfigured and in pain.

To tell a little of the story about me and my father less shyly, I would have to change the way I write. In real life, I experimented with homosexuality to break my pride, to open myself to the story.

I noticed a quick, deep change in Barry toward me when he realized that I had never lied to Ellen about my sexual past. Indeed, once or twice she corrected me when I answered a question of his inaccurately or too briefly. She had met everyone who had been in my life in the years before her, literary and ordinary and homosexual. None of them accepted her. Not one. She was pretty generally pounded after she ran off with me. Cautiously, Barry lectured me on how fortunate I was to have her. I said, in a slow-motion farce of obstinacy, "I know. What you don't know is that she was never this nice to me when I was well."

Isn't it a great swindle that your life matters to someone? That you're fighting a fight you are preordained to lose? That you're installed in a not entirely clean hospital? I signaled to Barry that I was still on my feet, still swinging, although of course I was supine— and pale green.

The actuality of AIDS as a complex (and complete) fatality produces in the patient a kind of detached wonderment at the doctor. If you are humane, what do you do when you are face-to-face with the depth of humiliation in the defeat? Like me, Barry could win only temporarily—why did he do it? Other doctors I have known hated death, *hated* it, couldn't bear to be near it except with a competitive advantage. Death and defeat are real downers—ask a pediatric neurologist who deals with mostly incurable conditions in children. I have seen, perhaps you have seen, a doctor weep with defeat. I am beyond the boundaries of myself as I pursue the thought, How does he do it?

Day to day, our compact, in this hospital room, is that we will skirt the unanswerable questions, deal in the terminology of details: the meaning of the blood tests, of the T-cell count, the presence of antigens and the nature of viral mutations and of bodily response, the effects of past events. My calcium, or something, has vanished. My blood pressure is dropping ominously. Barry is prescribing and dueling and countering. Medical decisions are made and a course is plotted, and all the while in the corner of the eye the outcome is glimpsed, the larger fate that is sometimes called destiny, coiled around the medical trajectory that is plotted on the insulted flesh.

It is odd to think of actual fate as being in constant motion inside you, but there it is—constantly pulling at you, constantly making you a target of ill luck or good luck. How badly suited I am for having a fate only Ellen knows. How damaged my body is by the virus only will become apparent at my death. The fundamental situation is all clarity and obscurity: a doomed boxing match with a submicroscopic virus that can have no real sense of the identity of its opponent and yet which, in its micro-ignorance, must win. It eats you alive. There is a tube in your nose, medicines drip and dissolve through the needles in your arms, partly banishing the specter of death (though not disfigurement); it peers at you from the dark corners of the room. One is something of a child again, afraid of the dark again.

And one is not. Long ago, in my late teens, I'd had a bad bout of pneumonia—brought on by malnutrition-as-rebellion when I was a sophomore at Harvard, and by the fact that I was so poor I'd had no winter clothes to take with me to school. I don't think I had ever been cold before, not like that. I'd gone home at Christmas to see my mother, my dying mother, and I remember taking a walk with her, and she said she'd been bored without me. That remark of hers, if I might be allowed to use Holden Caulfield's diction, killed me. That night the fever started and later, in my delirium, I said over and over, *I am dying.* (Maybe you even start to die, and then something saves you. Perhaps it's like flipping a coin or stepping off of a high, unrailed porch when you're first starting to walk, flinging the leg out into space . . . *Save my life* . . . Isn't that the core of childhood, that cry as you tip over and what will happen next?)

This time I am not risking delirium; I am too old. The mere fact of having AIDS is all the delirium I can manage. There are moments when I am even resorting to an as-if-ass-kissing mannerliness. It is an attempt to get on life's good side.

I know that I am working, fighting, enduring—the verbs change every few minutes—for the temporary survival of a part of myself, and that until now nothing was ever life-and-death for me, nothing that I can recall. Joe Brodkey would say I was unserious, the type to *walk into a hail of machine-gun bullets.* It was all a game, not hardball. *Everything is a game with you, Buddy.* Joe and Doris called me Buddy because they thought I looked like a movie star named Buddy Rogers who was married to Mary Pickford for a while. *Nothing really matters to you,* Doris had said. *You scare me. I think you died a long time ago. I think you died when your mother did, and all we ever got was a shadow who doesn't have enough sense to come in out of the rain.*

This time I have no time to be casual about it. But Barry, almost every day, twice a day, worriedly tells me that sooner or later I *will* crash, that I am not having one of the useful reactions to a diagnosis of pneumonia and AIDS. He shakes his head at my refusal to grieve—from what I can tell, he distrusts both one's denial of a private Utopianism and one's denial of death. "This is how I handle things," I tell him. Ellen is on Barry's side; she thinks I should give in and grieve. I am psychologically foreign to her. I feel she does not have a grasp of what is happening, of what my dying means, and how people will act. I myself am a coward, oversensitive, lazy, reclusive, but the mind and spirit have their requirement of independence.

The days pass. I do not die. Barry begins to show an increasing though still disbelieving respect for me, and for my *amusement* and my half-mocking politeness. After all, mine is a workable system. He creates a space for my tactics because I will not subscribe altogether to his. He talks to me; he meets me in my bleak no-man's land with charity. There, we confer on medical details, which remain mostly arcane to me, as I lie here with a half-dozen hematomas on each of my arms and a bedsore on my back.

The people I know who are addicted to rage are wretched. I am reminded of this now that we are playing hardball.

In certain variations of manner in Ellen and Barry and the nurses, I began to sense that the issue of immediate death had receded. And I was dimly aware—yet another symptom—that I was alive differently than before. I was alive in near-stillness while my wife and the doctor and the nurses had an enormous airflecked velocity about them: they had lifetimes to live.

Time was different, in a point-blank way. I was alive but it was not quite life I had returned to. Interesting, but dry. This was what my fate revealed to me now: that no one recovered from such a beating, from the knowledge of having been ruined. I was still, and would be, in danger of dying suddenly. Everything in the way of strength had been wiped away. I felt a corresponding increase of strength in everything around me, relative to me—planetary gravity, Ellen's breath, enemies' luck, the hypnotic emptiness of the light on the wall of the hospital room.

My friends and acquaintances who died of AIDS had near the end, most of them, an air of nervous pretense, like guarded actors. It was perhaps always clear, but so very clear to me now, that one plays a role in staying alive and that the place in which one plays this role is hollow, without a floor, without sensible definition. One plays this role with inverted brio, with a nonresident status one tries (and fails) to hide. I tried to hide it from Ellen. I was ghostly and could rustle and whisper. I could use my eyes and my smile—this is the actorly thing I saw in my friends—but the expression, the eyes, would misfire or go blank, go dark.

My dying parents had, I remembered, concentrated on one feature at a time, trying, in the fluster and ignorance of this last metamorphosis, to be grown-up dying people. This effort had had a quality of speech-making to it, and of modest vanity. Vanity is odd but medically encouraged. (I was termed *pale*, as in *pale lantern*. I believe I was actually gray-green. Ellen's small hands combed and brushed me.)

What I remembered of other terminal illnesses was how the human form had seemed to pulsate, like a fist opening and closing, moving back and forth from strength to weakness and then from lesser strength to greater weakness—the way the body would open as if into a palm, vulnerable, extended, and then reform into the fist in search of survival. Then, at some point, the fist would not reform itself, the pulsating would stop.

The trouble with death-at-your-doorstep is that it is happening to you. Also, that you are no longer the hero of your own story, no longer even the narrator. Barry was the hero of my story and Ellen the narrator. The tale was of my death amid others' lives—like a rock in a garden. I turned over in my hands the idea that I would not have an old age, that what was happening now *was* my old age. I would have no life to wake to except the unimaginably private one of the febrile genius that resides in dying. My private code, the actions of my past, what I had done, what had been done to me, all that was a physical and finite pattern now. I grinned inwardly at my nothingness, at the nothingness of my life. I had been a fool and weak. And subject to secret pieties. And I regretted that, but even the regret had no strength to it; it had a dryish, comic tone. It was awful. *Tell me, what were you doing all that time?* The questioning makes you bug-eyed. This line of inquiry is what some Christians call "embodiment"—the full earthly debt or burden or whatever you want to call it being shown to you. The condition pressed like a blade against every idea I had available; I was more oppressed now by defeat and the from-here-on-in than I had been by death sitting on my chest and asphyxiating me. I was a remnant of life, homeless psychically.

I longed for unbroken sleep. Barry and I glinted like

mirrors facing each other, me in my temporary, futile resuscitation, he in his very real and active splendor. He was watching me as carefully as ever; he still expected me to break down. *It is inevitable,* he said once.

I love Barry still, and I love my bit of remnant life. It is love without transcendence, however. One feels statistical probability in the limited taste of the air, the physical nature of the moments, the passage of time and the flitter of this edge of one's own remaining time. I love the mere passage of minutes, dry minutes scuttering. I love with distance, without energy; with the more and more amused almost-contempt of bystanderhood.

I don't want to praise death, but in immediacy death confers a certain beauty on one's hours—a beauty that may not resemble any other sort but that is overwhelming. Now, as death receded for a while, everything became rank disorder. The hospital jostled and jerked. The strain and rage of others grated and scraped on my heart. There was a woman in an adjacent room who insisted on screaming at the top of her lungs. She was told that this was very disturbing to the people around her (Ellen was beside herself), and she screamed that she didn't care. "I want to upset everyone," she paused to reply when the nurses tried to reason with her.

The smallest elements of existence were not possible without Ellen's help, even fixing the oxygen tube to my nose. She engineered the right-of-way minute by minute. She was at times egregiously imperfect—cranky if I woke her at night, prickly when I got tangled in the IV on the way to the bathroom—but the style of it was gentle. We fought over food: I wanted rich foods. My eating my first candy bar in three years was a bit funereal for her—Ellen *believes* in the macrobiotic diet. I believed my body's memory of health would be attached to the foods I had eaten for most of my life. I ate club sandwiches with bacon. I pointed out to her that we were attainted; I was, and she was through contact with me. We were hardly a glamorous pair anymore. "I look at it on the bright side," I said. "We are closer now to the worldwide statistical 'normal' than we ever were. Horrible deaths and total defeat are commonplace."

"The way you look on the bright side is strange, Harold," she said.

Such an opposition and interchangeability of wills is an old reality for us. Ellen believes in my judgment only perhaps by ignoring it much of the time. Head-on, when she asks my opinion, she invariably disbelieves what I say. *Oh no,* she says. I tend to be less sensible and less detailed than she is and much more dreamlike overall, which means that I believe in her judgment entirely too much or entirely too little no matter how hard I try to be exact toward her.

In the hospital, I couldn't rest without her protection or eat or drink or go to the john without her help. It's not so different from being in love, this dependence; it is exaggerated, yet not unfamiliar. We usually slept at alternate times, in a form of mutual permission and involvement. (This, too, was familiar. We had never been in sync at home: I snored and woke often, especially when I was writing, while Ellen slept soundly and hardly moved nightlong. We woke differently, too, and at different hours.)

I had done stuff of the sort she did for me for my parents, but the tones and the humors were different. Take the matter of thought, of trying to think: I used her will, her sense of coherence if I wanted to comprehend anything. And—literally—I hadn't the strength to finish a thought without her help; it took two of us to carry a thought. She guessed at my purpose and knew my old thoughts about the nature of the world and my style, and she patched things together for me. And, as she began to tire in the circumstances of hospital treatment and the ailment, I became more sharply crippled.

Many of the hospital workers I met were women, and over time I chatted with them a bit, though I was shy and self-conscious, ashamed that my blood represented a risk. And they spoke, most of them, of the difficulties of working among women—the competition that went on, and the class and ethnic warfare, the assertions of pride and the inventive modes of halfway being on strike. I started to mentally record which of the nurses and nurses' aides and cleaning women judged themselves more by the work itself and which put the social ranking of the workplace first. I thought about how the women in my field of work, in literary work, were divided in that way. There was little else to concentrate on, unless you counted the occasional open combat outside the room, or someone weeping in the corridor, or the screamer. I didn't want the children to see me here. Ellen and I had not yet told anyone in the family; we hadn't the energy to face the children. We hadn't turned to our lawyer or my agent because, to be honest, I was not eager to have them comment on our situation. Friends, either. Besides, if we hadn't talked to the children, we couldn't very well turn to friends first and have the children learn later that we had distrusted their reaction.

In some cases, I had specific reasons: This grown child or this friend was about to move. That friend was giving a wedding or working very hard or was recovering from the recent death of someone. Beneath these reasons, I did not want to invite trespass. I had no wish to put my fevers and cold clamminess and great helplessness on exhibit. I did not want my drowned, limp, whispering self magnified into anecdote. I did not want to be goaded into the effort of public behavior. (I could apologetically claim that I had no strength to show gratitude if people were kind.) The collective vigor of the people we were close to—well, if they should form a phalanx of wills, as seemed inevitable, then I would have to adopt their definitions of my predicament. It seemed too messy and difficult to speak of any of this, or to speak and omit this, or to ask Ellen to speak to everyone for me.

But my own say-so rested on Ellen's strength, which was lessening under the strain. I thought she and I should go home and be alone there. One morning, I yelled at Barry. My voice came out in the whisper left to me after a bronchoscopy. He leaned forward and made a face to show he hadn't heard. Ellen repeated it, rephrased, for me: "You've done wonders for me, but I can't manage the hospital." He argued back, using statistics. To combat *Pneumocystis*, Bactrim was being administered to me intravenously via a machine that ticked and beeped it slowly into the bloodstream. I needed to stay on it for a while longer, even though my body could barely tolerate it. Barry said it wasn't feasible to try to take it at home, given the side effects.

Do you know the feeling of dismay when you can't phrase an argument? I said that I was old, that we were shattered figures, and that I needed to sleep and dream. That it couldn't matter much where I was. Ellen translated for me, but in the middle, she began to weep silently. Barry nodded shrewdly, gave me a brilliant smile, then a worried look, and then began to describe my state in fairly dire and professional terms—an argument for staying in the hospital. Responding to my anger, he said he had never colored his speeches, never encouraged me to have false hope.

I said, "You color everything you say to me."

Ellen looked neutral; she wouldn't support me on that.

Barry then said in a serious tone, a bit tired, something about never having said to me that it would be easy now or ever again, never having said it would not be a bad death. The phrase he used was "a difficult death." I went crazy inside hearing him, crazed with grief for myself.

Ellen sat rigidly and looked calm and blank.

"Barry," I said, "we can't hack it here. We have to

sell a house we have in the mountains. I've got to redo my will. We've got to tell the children. And we're not going to tell them from here or have them see me with tubes up my nose in a none-too-clean room. And I have to write letters to some people to tell them. And I have to work—I have to."

Barry's shoulders sagged a bit. He smiled. "You have a peculiar attitude toward this thing." Toward AIDS, he meant. Or dying.

"It's probably the prednisone," I said.

He had a certain respect for the differences in kind between him and me. And he knew Ellen by now. He stood there studyingly. He looked inside his head, then he said he had to go off and look at the charts. He came back in ten minutes or so and said he'd begin tapering off some of the medication, and he would see to it that we could leave as soon as the tests showed—I forget what.

I thought at first Barry lied and did not reduce the medication, or not by much. But after a few days it was obvious that he had, and I believed he was working toward Ellen's and my going home. Ellen watched the sense of helpless stillness occur and reoccur in me once or twice an hour, so many times that it was the best description overall of my condition, this helplessness.

When Barry entered the room, I would brighten argumentatively.

"You're getting better," he said. "You're coming along. There's a lot of life in the old guy yet."

"So we have come to the edge of the light at the end of the tunnel, have we?"

"Is he always this impossible?" he said to Ellen gaily.

"Usually, he's worse," she said. "He likes you."

"Help me, Barry. I want to go home."

"Friday," he said. This was on a Tuesday. "If everything goes all right, Friday."

I said, a fool and macho, "Friday, OK. But I'm leaving on Friday no matter what. I'll walk out of here no matter what's going on."

"You won't be able to walk," he said in a sudden burst of semi-intimate, semi-brutal humor.

I knew I did not want to live or die or suffer or continue *in any way* with Ellen inside the hospital. The hospital is like a bus terminal on a weekend, full of mad and abominable and listless human goods in transit. Going home was an idea, my idea, and it became the germ of a story that was mine once again. The only way conscious language can deal with wild variability is by telling a story in reference to real time. This was my story: I had come to the end of Ellen's strength, and it was time to go home.

~~~

As I said, to die of AIDS is to die outside a tradition, in a silence of sorts. The social horror of having AIDS in America—Barry referred to it in a peculiarly impressive and emphatic way, indirectly, by saying that it was, of course, advisable for me to keep it a secret: "No one can handle it. Everybody changes. You have enough to deal with."

"I am fatally ill *anyway.* . . ." (Ellen's gestures were spotlit for me; she was staring at the wall, because the word *fatally* so affected her.)

"Believe me, you can have a couple of good years. But there are other problems. I have a patient . . ." He spoke of a youngish woman with AIDS who had a husband and two children; none of them was infected. This woman told a close friend who lived in her building and whose children played with her children. "And everything is changed . . . even among the children. She shouldn't have told that woman."

Barry started giving Ellen advice on which drugstores were "discreet." I realized that part of what made her look so strained was the certain way wickedness registers on her face. You might call it her startled liberal's expression. Barry asked me to consider staying in the hospital a while longer. I listed on the wretchedly

unanatomical bed, studied the unnecessarily rotten
food, surveyed the vast psychological loneliness and dis-
placement and disorientation of the other patients,
whom I met when I walked up and down the corridor in
rehearsal for escape from the hospital. It hurt to be
there. I was only pretending to be brave, after all.

I yearned for passivity but was incapable of it. Nature
sees to it that we go a little mad with action in childbirth
or in battle, and we stop fearing death—and then are
surprised by it. I felt a self-willed madness of action
settle over me as a form of anesthesia; I watched my
mind lapse into an intoxicated sense of death as a Very
American Thing, which is to say, requiring firm negotia-
tion. I needed to make arrangements about editing the
last hundred pages of *Profane Friendship*. Also, I had
started a long novel about dying as seen by a young man,
and it was far enough along that I wanted to take
another look and see if I was sufficiently strong to finish
it. For most of each night, partly because of the dangers,
partly because of the comparative silence, I lay still or
sat up now, the oxygen tube in my nose, and tried to
think what to do, and what to think.

I found myself dry and ordinary. Yet now, when I
slept, I began to dream things I could remember. At first
my dreams were blackish and skimpy. I awoke with a
sense of returning from a pool of ink, semi-melted

newsprint, something censored, excised. Soon the dreams involved vacations and visits and sweetness and ease that turned to unease. I would be prying and exploring a wall, for instance, a wall that opened in accordion folds and then made a slow, excited swing out over a cliff and glinting, restless water—and it would dawn on me that this slow, sweet excitement was fatal, final.

In other dreams, cliffs collapsed and bridges, too, and I fell. An enormous, slow-moving dark bird with a fanciful tail larger than itself flew above me as I dropped toward the water, through a soft, lucid space, in a foreignness of being unsupported, unsafe.

I suppose the vacation thing in my dreams had to do with my not writing now, with inactivity as escape, with the end of duty and the pleasures of a life. Fighting *the good fight*—as Miss Van Matre taught me in the fourth grade—for truth and justice and order was over. That absurd, cruel recruitment was finished. The self freed from duty—in immense, simple truancy—floats and gloats.

Awake, I talked in a whisper, and the weakening Ellen listened in a passion of perfect listening, with a fine quickness in comprehension of the syllables and syntax—it showed in her eyelids, in flashes of *signal received*. Ellen has always talked differently from me, in summaries, in a socially practiced style, not showy, not always confident, but bold. We had talked across gulfs, across the differences in our histories, in our gender. In the past, we had in fact often faked the need to talk, the number of emergencies we claimed had to be dealt with in words. In the hospital room, that habitual pretense took on a certain frayed, hunted quality, as we talked between interruptions by the staff.

She did not stay with me because of warmth between us: I was far too weak, far too limited to feel affection except as a distant measure of what was going to happen to me now. Love? How do you love in this condition? I called Ellen an ass and a dolt; I told her that illness and death are a divorce anyway. She ignored me.

She did not stay for lack of other choices. We had enough money that we could have hired a private nurse for a while (and there are charities and charitable people and friends).

She did not leave me; she stayed and listened to me struggle to speak.

I suppose my predicament affected the span or reach of her intelligence. For her to be near me in the way she was near me, all day and all night, was like being in a hole in the ground, without any range of vision. If I had wept or cried out with the pain or despair of death, or passionately inveighed against the treatment, she would have been set free in a sense, though she would have had to bear that horror. Perhaps I did not really want to set her free.

She was afraid I felt too much alone, and so she kept offering me her life. I took it, not always gratefully. I am claustrophobic, or was, and I had confessed one night a few years back that I hated the idea of the solitude in a coffin. And she'd said, "Well, we can be buried in the same coffin, a double coffin." She brought that up again, and she told me over and over that I was a wonderful and a great writer and that she loved me.

When she slept, I arranged myself in my stiff posture—I still could not straighten my back or shoulders, the pressure and tightness in my lungs were too great—and tried to think about the soft-lipped sad universe with so much death in it. But no thoughts came. I felt no Presence, only her presence. At times, in the dark—or with the light on, while Ellen slept—I struggled to figure out why the extreme nature of my predicament never, for a minute, took top rank; why Ellen was in the way.

When we first met, Ellen told me that she had learned through being a mother how to be strong, and I didn't believe her. She had been surrounded by difficulties and threats and lies and by assaults on the soul—the usual domestic and familial things where women are concerned. She had been profoundly unhappy, but she had managed. This experience of crazed survival might define a woman's citizenship in the world, but to me it seemed impossible that it could have produced the strength of this fine-spun, quick-witted woman who offered such goodness as a part of courtship.

She said now, "When I think of your life, of your not having your own mother, and now this . . ." And I finally understood what she meant by saying she had learned her strength as a mother; that this was a love in spite of almost everything, with quite a lot of forgiveness mixed in. It is really quite terrifying, a good woman, a sexual one, offering and giving you fragments of motherhood that you have never had.

She had run off with me. And (I repeat) when her son had been ill, no one from her previous life had truly helped her. You cannot imagine how wounded she was by his illness, a slow-growing cancer he had had perhaps from the time he was ten years old. And since the possibility of illness is always there still, shadowing his life, she could not forget this.

Ellen and her son had had to measure the uses of truths and of partial truths. They had learned to read indications of character in doctors. Ellen had had to measure what her son said and what the doctors said and what her ex-husband said. And what I said. Sometimes she had had to guess. In the end, she was the only one the boy trusted.

She and her son had arrived at certain principles of how to proceed. They worked out some theoretical notions about illness, some of which were not so far from the literary and philosophical notions on which my work depended. In that sense we now had a new shared language, and she used it to ease my loneliness. She kept saying how well my ideas worked out in regard to AIDS. I think I sometimes imitated her son in how I acted.

Christ, how glad I was that she was with me now and at the same time how much I wanted to spare her all of this shit. I told her I wanted her to hire someone to take care of me, that I wanted her to distance herself from me—from my defeat.

"I don't want Barry to keep me here, and he might on the ground that I'm so helpless. And he'll listen to you. I don't want to alienate him—he's the doctor I want. But he knows you can't nurse me through these next months."

Ellen said, "I don't want to hire anyone, a stranger in the apartment. I'm strong. I'm macrobiotic."

"Look, I need a nurse I can order around."

She set her face; she sat in a very erect posture. "You can order me around."

"That would be a change." No one ever ordered her around. (She could be manipulated. Her three children or her four grandchildren sometimes came at her from all angles, and she went along with it.)

I figured she'd get tired of nursing me—everyone gets tired of nursing anyone—and then we'd hire someone. When I ran out of money, I'd kill myself.

"Then let's go home tomorrow," I said. "No more delays."

"I'm ready to go home anytime."

But Barry dawdled and said it would take another weekend, perhaps even a week. I blew up at him in my whisper. I told him he was a damn fool to have prescribed such heavy medication. I told him, for the tenth time, that the room was unbearably ugly, the bed useless for sleeping, the food vile, the nights oppressive and close to terrifying. That is, if I let Ellen sleep. I wanted to go home and die there or recuperate there to whatever degree I could. I wanted to sleep and to dream. I wanted to have the most interesting illness, if not in my apartment house, then at least in my apartment. I was tired of being unimportant. I wanted to exert my will or be utterly without will, and I couldn't do either in the hospital. I promised to stay on the medications. I said I would make an effort to live. I said I would refuse to speak or respond in any way to anyone in the hospital (but him and Ellen) until my IV was unplugged. "I've had enough. Nothing is left of me, nothing. Nothing in my body is functioning anymore. I do thank you for saving my life and all that, but enough is enough."

Barry looked at Ellen. "He's not exaggerating," she said.

I think this was the moment of the beginning of friendship; I mean, he did what I asked, or asked obliquely—that we might share a mutual truth about the actual reality here. But his truth was purposeful: he wanted to expand the time I had, while I had lost my sense of the future.

I believe that in the end it is sorrow over the world and over being disbelieved that kills us. It is the recognition of one's actual truth, the truth of one's actual life, that is so life-giving. And Barry changed in his own notions about what was best for me; he saw it more and more in terms of us, of Ellen and me, to such an extent that he began to tell her what I should do medically, and I could close my eyes and rest while he did it.

"You can go home," he said. "But you will be weak, weaker than you think, than you ever imagined." He paused. Then: "It takes four to six months to get over the pneumonia." He said I had a number of factors in my favor, Ellen in particular, and he sort of semi-bowed

to her. She looked stern and nurselike. He said that
what might happen next—he meant bits of cancer and
other infections—he could control with drugs, with
medication.

I said, "For a while."

He said, "You've done better than predicted. You
probably had the pneumonia for months, maybe half a
year. Your vital signs aren't at all bad. You're a pretty
strong guy."

Ellen said, "He has a strong constitution."

Barry addressed himself to that and to other matters. He reminded Ellen of the importance of keeping
latex gloves handy and what to do in case of a blood
spill. As he spoke he grew distant. He retreated again
into a medical perspective. He was saying good-bye; I
think he assumed I would adopt an alternative form of
treatment and would come to him only when an infection loomed. And death. He repeated that the overwhelming majority of middle-class AIDS patients keep it
secret that they have the disease. He repeated that I
needed another "few days" of serious medication; it
would be better to wait through the next weekend at
least.

I said, "Never." Then, because he was in the mood he
was in, I said: "Tell me how I'm going to die." *You don't*

want to know was what I read in his expression. But I did not particularly want to die entirely inside the vocabulary and mood of AIDS and outside the line of traditional deaths in my family. Meanwhile, I wasn't smart enough or strong enough to figure out for myself when the horrors would start.

"We'll think about that part later. You can have a few very, very good years," Barry said.

Ellen started to ask him about nutrition, about ten-year survivors and the possibility of mysterious cures.

"Shut up," I told her. I said to Barry, "Five years is statistically rare, right?"

"Yes."

"Am I going to choke to death?"

"I don't know."

"But you can *half*-promise that at the end of six months, I'll feel human? And have a good chance at two more years?"

"Sure. Yes. A lot of people have a wonderful time."

"In other words, maybe no."

"I don't know."

"Well, there we are," I said.

"If you stay in for another four or five days we can—"

And Ellen started in again, this time on exercise and the right climate, on long-range hope.

Barry said nothing. He just looked at her with affection.

I said, "Ellen, can it. The wages of sin, of sexual canoodling, is no miracles. Anyway, it's less strain; no miracles, I mean."

"Barry, tell him that nutrition matters. At least, make him give up sugar."

"How miserable am I going to be?" I asked him.

Barry said, "We have medicines now, we have backup medicines. We can keep you alive *for a while*. You're one of the lucky ones—you're not alone, you're not carrying half a dozen diseases." He wanted me to have that respite. He kept trying to describe it. I taunted him.

"You sound like a brochure."

He was offering a gift, like someone telling you about a good review, an honest one, or someone offering you an actually sensible thought about something you care about. Doctors will tell you that bad news kills people with AIDS and that certain managerially assertive personalities seem to survive past the statistical average.

"Tell her there's no hope and that I can eat anything I want, it doesn't matter."

Barry said to Ellen, "I want him to gain weight, whatever that takes."

"Barry!"

"I'm not against good nutrition, but weight *is* an

issue," he said to Ellen, who put on a brave air. He then said to me, "Don't be surprised at how lousy you feel."

I had thought he was being careless of me in his gambling attempt to get me past the pneumonia, but he had been gambling intelligently, of course. I had also been upset by the crude, uneven way the medication had at times been administered, and by the fact that he often hadn't been there to watch over me. I admitted as much, admitted that it was the psychological loneliness of feeling disposable, of being singled out for mistreatment in a country of normalcy. I promised to behave and not shame him by giving up or by committing suicide right away.

He sort of stammered. "Don't be surprised—don't be surprised if you can't *do* much at first. But hang on." That air of saying good-bye hovered around us again. "If you crash, we have pills—we'll get you mood-elevators. Whatever you need to know, you can ask me at any time."

"Well, thanks. You saved my life. Of course, that's not saying much—the whole thing is a mess, Barry."

"Outlook is important. It affects the white cells. I can recommend a psychotherapist who has experience with AIDS—"

I partly understood that he thought I was angry with him and with the disease and was in despair.

"Outlook isn't a simple matter. I want control of my mind. And a modicum of rationality. I feel like shit. And I want to sleep. I want to sleep in a decent bed."

He gave me a look of niceness that was also another grim signal. "You should start on AZT now," he said. He told me the semi-encouraging figures on AZT and full-blown AIDS.

"Don't buy it in your neighborhood: it's only used for AIDS and HIV, and people will know. I'll give Ellen the name of a drugstore in midtown. It has a good stock of the medicines you'll need, and it's well priced."

I had a sense, perhaps gray and without color, perhaps without wording—unless you want to call inward cries and inward gasps of shock hidden from others a form of words—I had a sense of Barry retreating. He had hospital duties, gravely ill patients. But it was more than that. Perhaps he saw naked pride and helplessness and the end.

My sense was that he was making room for a dying man. For the operations of ego and will of a dying man. He knew, better than I did, what I was going to suffer in the next weeks and months. He was showing medical knowledge and respect in a revised etiquette of permission—the permission I was asking for.

I knew that I wasn't leaving him, I was leaving the hospital. Although I might leave him, depending on what I learned if I lived. I hadn't a clear idea of the middle areas and the real extent of the humiliation of dying—humiliation in regard to the world. Barry knew I would discover it soon. The world is far worse than a hospital.

1 could hardly admit to the simplicity of his response: it was that he truly pitied me, Ellen and me. He pitied us.

Ellen went around the hospital floor saying good-bye to some of the nurses and nurses' aides. I didn't say good-bye to anyone; I sat up in bed, shoeless but otherwise dressed, utterly silent, not moving. Ellen returned, and I stood up without much breath—there was a good deal of gasping, as if the room were filled with startled crows.

I was dimly aware of the horror and unease Ellen felt at my state, but I couldn't afford to recognize it for what it was. I would have foundered. I was upright and in motion with only a small margin between me and fainting. She helped me into a wheelchair. I joked about always having wanted a wheelchair of my own, but that upset her. She doesn't snap at people, but she spoke a bit sharply to me now. I didn't want to know that she was worried about pushing her husband in a wheelchair out of the hospital. I told her, not seriously, that she pushed

it too pathetically. The nurses had arranged for an
orderly, and he showed up then and whirled the chair
along with vast energy and youth. Tired as I was, wiped
out and skewed, I felt that terrible amusement again,
this time at being whirled along.

Outside the hospital, the light had a perceptible
weight, and I blinked and flinched. The outdoor noises,
city noises, flew and scratched. I struggled to control my
breathing so that Ellen would not sense my panic at
being overcome by noise and light. And it was as Barry
had said: I had not really known how sick I was—dying,
yes, but not how sick.

I felt myself dissolve into the space spreading around
me. In the taxicab, in the streets, I was so crippled by
filmy fluctuations of consciousness—on East Seventy-
second, on Madison, on West Eighty-sixth, where the
walls of brownstones seemed watery and then gauzy—
that I was far more imprisoned by weakness than I had
been by the hospital and its routines. I knew right away I
had made a mistake in forcing Barry to let me leave the
hospital a few days early, but I also knew it was possible
to be mistaken and to be right. I was maddened by my
silent passing out and coming to in the city stink as the
taxi bounded and bounced. I stayed upright. Ellen was
stiff-faced and brightly talkative beside me. "I can't
respond," I whispered. She held my hand. Halfway home,

I was so ill with exhaustion that tears of pain came to my eyes. I had no intention of acknowledging my mistake. I said, at least half a dozen times, "Boy, is it wonderful to be out of the hospital." Then I gave that up and asked Ellen if she was managing, or if this was too much for her. If she had said yes, I would have turned back. She said she was OK.

We, I, made it to the apartment, and I climbed into my bed in my clothes. Ellen undressed me, set out the pills and the notebook in which she was going to log my symptoms and the hours at which I took the pills. The apartment has double-hung windows and wall-to-wall industrial carpeting to cut down noise. Still, it is noisy compared with the country. And quiet compared with the hospital.

I dozed and woke, but uncomfortably and without being refreshed by the sleep, which was as truly terrifying as falling off the edge of the world might be—to be so unrefreshed by sleep. I walked, crept, partly crawled to the stereo in my darkened bedroom and played one of Bach's partitas; it sounded harsh to me. I slept, always in an uncurative way, sometimes with music playing. Much of the time I just listened to the sounds of distant street noises and of Ellen coming and going.

I had the beginnings of a violently bad reaction to a Bactrim pill. I blew up into a purple rash and fever. I cursed Barry, but the rate of effectuality for Bactrim is more than 95 percent, so I would probably have to try it again later. (The AZT made me ill, too, but I felt it forming something like a nearly transparent wall between me and the virus.) Sick and weak, each day, in the morning, for an hour or more, I stirred myself and worked on the last draft of the Venice book. Red and covered with spots (allergy to the drugs), I worked, and while I worked I felt nothing apart from a weakness of mind and some nausea. I mean, I had no reaction to the story or to the prose: I had to work with memories of response.

Sometimes I couldn't work at all, couldn't focus, and I would cry, but only a bit, and crawl back to bed, or if I was working in bed I would cover my eyes with my hands and lie still and breathe and doze and then try again to work. I must admit I felt truly accursed. My mother, my real mother, died, according to family accounts, of a curse laid on her by her father, a wonder-working rabbi. When I was barely two, she died painfully, over a period of months, either of peritonitis from a bungled abortion or from cancer, depending on who related the story. Then Doris, my father's cousin, and Joe came for me and, later on, adopted me. I was told that Doris took me once to the hospital to see my mother, who smelled of infection and medicines and that I refused her embrace, clinging instead to the perfumed Doris; the rescued child was apparently without memory of the dying mother. (Perhaps that was the real crime, and not my obduracy with Joe.) So, in between working out when I could most probably have become infected with AIDS, I fell into a mood of being accursed, of being part of an endless family story of woe and horror.

I felt worse each day, almost as if as the emergency faded so did the mobilized strength. Endless sickness without death is more sickening than I would have imagined. I wanted to make, as a sort of joke, a version of the superhuman effort that Ellen wished for from me. But, you know, as you get older you get worn out in regard to superhuman efforts—you've made them for your child or in your work (superhuman for you) or in sport or love or for someone who is ill. And then the possibility is gone. Ellen was working at a superhuman rate, nursing me, helping me up and to the word processor and back to bed. She shopped, cooked, kept house, took care of pending business, dealt with whatever emergencies came up, answered the phone and lied to people about my illness, fed us and made conversation, and proofread the work I produced. She got us movies for the VCR and lay down with me and kept me company, and brought me ice bags when the fever rose and my head hurt, and kept the medication log and saw to it that I took the medications and my temperature when I was supposed to, and, when I asked her to, she sang to me.

She helped me dress and then undress; she didn't approve of my staying in pajamas all day. Her omnipotence was at full stretch during this period, which lasted perhaps five weeks, and had a softly shining and rather detached aura to it that enclosed my sense of being accursed and diluted. It was a cousin to that neurotic activity of will in able women which is so often written about with disapproval, and it was crazed, I suppose, that tirelessness, that as-if inexhaustible tenderness. Clearly forced, or maybe not, it was far stronger and more unflagging in effect than any courtship intensity that had ever been directed at me.

We called no one. We were still telling the family and anyone else who telephoned that I had pneumonia, nothing more. In a rather transparent isolation, my arrogant deathliness and her burning gentleness were dancing together in a New York light in our apartment. This was like childhood, a form of playing house.

Then she said, "When are we going to tell the children?" She wasn't looking forward to it—it's not just embarrassment, you know: it's preliminary distress in case they're not very nice at first; and, on the other hand, as a parent you are ashamed to inflict this downer on them if they are warmhearted and do sympathize. The likeliest thing is that you'll have to console them.

"Later. In a few days, we'll start. I can't deal with it yet."

"That's all right."

She was careful, so that I would not blame myself. I felt myself to be thoroughly repellent. I had disowned my body now and was mostly pain and odors, halting speech and a sick man's glances. The truths in such domestic and emotional enclosures tend to go unrecorded. Things drift into the sanctuary from the outer world; the television is a window, and the telephone is a murmurous keyhole. Somewhere in this phantasmagoria, Ellen decided to wake me.

A kiss—how strange her lips felt, and the quality of life in them. Of course, I thought, of course. The sense I had of her, the sensations: the heat of her skin, the heat of her eyes so close to me, everything in her was alive still and full of the silent speeches that life makes. She was warm and full of responsive motion. My lips and feelings had the deadness of a sullen child's.

I accepted her and her affection as truth, as being as much truth along those lines as I was likely to want. This meant that by the second week I was home we both realized that, in this limited world of mutual watchfulness and of unselfishness-for-a-while, this period was for us, in awful parody, honeymoonlike, and that this was acceptable to both of us, grief or death at the end or not.

Grief aside, nothing ugly happened at all. Since she didn't mind—or rather didn't show disgust at my ashenness—I grew more affectionate: the corpse put his arm around her. She noticed and commented on the strength of my heartbeat.

"Yes, I've always been especially proud of my heartbeat."

She kissed me on the lips with generous marks of interest and amusement. She said to me, "No one would believe that this was one of the happiest times of my life."

I roared with laughter, which hurt my stiff lung and made me choke. And I came alive again, for a little while. Well, why not? When the other things are over and done with, when savagery and silence are the impolite, real thing, you're not alone. You still pass as human among humans. There are things that have to be done, family things, literary stuff, things having to do with AIDS. I do them with her marks of interest and amusement on my face.

Summer 1993

Dying, too, has a certain rhythm to it. It slows and quickens. Very little matters, but that little is of commanding importance to me. I feel the silence ahead of me as I have all my life felt the silence of God as a given and a source of reasonable terror. This is something one must bear, beyond the claims of religion, not the idea of one's dying but the reality of one's death. One schools oneself in an acceptance of the terror. It is the shape that life takes toward its end. It is a form of life.

By mid-June it was time to tell the children. Ellen and I have four children and seven grandchildren between us. They were too sentimental and upset by the bad luck at first. They cared too much. But no one rebuked us.

"Oh, poor Daddy," my daughter said. I said she was welcome to be horrified and ground down by this news, and I would be patient with her feeling like that. She said it was not a horror, but: "Who am I going to talk to? I'm not through with you."

One of the worst moments came during a visit from my grandson Abner, aged four, a wide-faced blond, a second child, bright, and rather expert at emotional warfare. I hadn't seen him in four months, and he looked at me snottily and said, "I don't remember *you*." I said, "I used to be a pink-and-black horse." He looked at me, thought or reacted, then grinned and said, "I remember you now," and came over and took my hand and generally didn't leave my side. But the horror was I had no strength to respond or pretend after only a short while, less than an hour. I am not able to be present for him and never will be anymore. That led to a bad twenty-four hours.

As the weeks passed, I began to concentrate on what was going on physically inside me. As Barry had predicted, the getting better was so slow, the increment of strength each day was so slight that it, too, weighed on me—the paltriness of the success. But after a while I could walk around the block once and sometimes twice a day, using a cane. I slept a lot, I ate rich food and gained weight. I worked. I had a lousy disease and was, perhaps, a pariah. On the other hand, I had a new novel, I had Ellen, I had a fantastic doctor—and with these pieces I wasn't, oh, socially wiped out. I wasn't bankrupt. We talked about the possibility of buying a dog as soon as my breathing improved. We had already bought a new, truly good television set (pop culture is unbearable when it is not superlatively presented in all its dexterities and grandeurs). This is how one prepares to endure a terminal illness.

You see, it was all very middle class—grievous, of course, frightening, but privileged. It was a happy ending, I mean for a while. Like all middle-class happy endings. You get a middle-class happy ending only for a little while anyway.

It's never easy to talk to someone who's ill. In the country, in the mountains, where we have come as we used to do, 220-pound Bruce Feml and unsmiling Hillard Hommel and the others, the lot of them churchgoers and old, blink, brighten ambiguously, stare a bit, and wave. And when they speak there is an indication that morally they do not approve but that they will not

discard me either. A lot of the men I see as I blunder
on about my business are not hate-filled, although I
am Death, Death and Punishment-for-Sin. Some of the
vacationing class of people of the enclaves up here are
more self-conscious, even flirtatious: sly and oblique.
Some men stare me in the eye and often, even casually,
reveal a thin border of scandal in their own families.

Barry was so encouraging after my last visit that yesterday, when we arrived in the country, in the cooler
air—with a fine wind blowing and the stodgy trees
attempting witty movements, and with the monkshood
in bloom, very tall purple panicles next to our stone
wall—I went entirely mad, carrying things, charging up
and down stairs, and then collapsed, not seriously but
totally, for eighteen hours. But I went on feeling happy
and released.

I am eleven pounds heavier than when I left the hospital in early May. Now, in the country, I can stand
straighter; my breathing isn't so noisy. I am not in
despair or cracked open. Or drastically humbled. And
sometimes when I first wake up I do feel my body as
I used to feel it when awake when I was younger, that
odd, flexible, long-limbed *extent* of reliability and all the
tubes of sensation flashed a little in a silent fusillade,
and, in private, one stretched in a courtship display.
That old sense of luck, of at-least-I-have-this-whatever-

else-happens, returns but not in that verb tense. I feel myself to be smoke. Or when my eye catches part of the arc of flight of a bird, I feel myself shiver and swiftly break into clusters of flight. Sometimes the wind seems to enter me.

Most of the men I know, straight or otherwise, still say I have been lucky, that I seem lucky to them. It is tucked in among other remarks. One of them, who has not written me, made such an issue of my *luck* as an excuse for his abandoning my books that he said it was the reason he could not defend my work at any length. I did, for a while, truly despise him. "You like your wife," he muttered. "You can live with her. . . . That is unforgivable."

We have a large, wooden, many-windowed house in an enclave of ninety such wooden houses, most of them built at the end of the nineteenth century with a certain architectural exuberance of that time, the houses cantilevered often or perched on the side of an old, worn-down mountain overlooking a gorge—a much-painted mountain pass: *The Way West* or *Kaaterskill Falls* such pictures were usually called. The chief road in goes over a stone bridge that sails atop an eighty-foot waterfall. The air is pure, constantly shifting as always in a mountain pass; the walls of the pass form sluices and channels for the perpetual shifts of weather. The house is a folly: it has seventy-five windows. I am not the only dying man in The Park, as it is called. A man a few houses down who is in his seventies is terminal with lung cancer. He is a greenish skull, and when he appears in public he is angry and makes violent grimaces: "Life is pain," he said to me.

As I write this there is a slight breeze outside, and what is framed in the window, the square of green mountainside, is fluttering like an eyelid.

Can anyone understand the particularity of fate? Barry says one ought to mimic ordinary life, one's life from before. Pretending to be well or half-well would tear me apart. Perhaps such pretense helps young people with AIDS keep going—I am one of the oldest patients Barry has treated.

One's life from before. Only a half year ago, at the end of January there was our homecoming to New York after three months abroad. I, a tall, discomfited couch potato emerging from a medium-sized jet, that flying slum. I can remember reentry, having to set in place the intricate system of assertions and responses, the mental and physical aggressions, that are necessary in New York.

Each place Ellen and I had gone to—Berlin, Venice, Rome—has its own inner systems of interlocking aggressions and violences, its famous culture of them. I became attuned to the gladiatorial spirit at Rome's Fiumicino Airport and to the grim, order-giving xenophobia at Tegel, in Berlin. New York systems don't work in those towns—you get out of practice with New York systems, unless you stay in hotels that specialize in your class and nationality. But if you've been a tourist immersed in other places, the return to Manhattan, the home ghetto of choice—bitter cabdrivers, high-pressure face-lifted old ladies, mad landlords—it's like being dipped in hell, especially when you're jet-lagged.

The self-assertion of the locals is part of the mystic wonder of the place. And this begins in the overwhelmingly strange experience of using a New York airport. What do you suppose makes the customs guards and the guides who indicate which window you go to with your passport look so sad? The aggressions of ethnic groups begin at Kennedy, too. This time, a flying squad of Wasp heroines pushed into the line of people waiting for taxis and had to be chased off by a Russian-speaker in a golfing hat and Day-Glo wheelchair with a phenomenally militant sense of justice. Earlier, Italians had been taking over the best places along the conveyor belt, elbowing you, looking at you piteously. And the silently

angry French people in really good clothes had been cutting across your path with their luggage carts.

If your taxi driver is not aggressive, you will never get
out of Kennedy Airport. People shamelessly block the
crosswalks and ignore the lights. No one cooperates.
Kind liberals in cars who refuse to edge forward into this
shameless mass cause gridlock at the intersections.
Then, the visual blight along the highway has behind it
the great secret that a glimpse of the incredible Manhattan skyline is coming—the towers under a large sky,
airplane-dotted, and with wheeling seabirds, and
bustling with clouds and light, including a glowing pale-
yellow corona of pollution around the towers themselves.

In narrow side streets and at the lights occur traffic
confrontations, negotiations, bluster, and jockeying.
Surely treeless Manhattan is the home of the bald ego,
the American national bird. Different styles of aggres-
sion seem to be basic to gender. The virility syndrome is
different from the exoticism of the being-not-male-and-
to-be-looked-at syndrome that women labor under. New
York women either deny or exaggerate the exoticism
element. Denial and exaggeration, and male and female
distrust of them, underlie much of New York psychoana-
lytic culture. But what is most striking on returning
after a long absence is the extreme obviousness of male
assertion, beginning with the size and shape of the sky-

scrapers, and how male and female pretension both suffer in some kind of permanent crisis. It is almost impossible in New York to be rich enough for comfort in regard to your own gender. You have to be so rich—as in having your own plane and chauffeur—that you are part of the general scene in only a small, glancing way. But those of us who are not that rich do not exactly return to New York, either. We return to a fortress segment of it, a willfully isolated, specialized part of it.

Drenched in momentary inadequacy and adrenaline, I arrived at my apartment house. The doorman on duty was the Hindu guy. The Guatemalan doorman of the earlier shift was just leaving, dressed in his helmet and quilted Tyvek jacket; he has a BMW motorcycle. The Romanian doorman, who had our mailbox key, wasn't there. The boiler was "half broken." Polish workmen were pounding on the roof. The Sunday *Times* when I bought it was missing the book review and style sections, which I took as advice on what not to bother reading. The local macrobiotic restaurant was crowded with people dealing macrobiotically with the virility and exoticism factors. The wind was cold and aggressive.

Anton, the Romanian doorman, is a genuinely competitive human being. He has about as much sense of social class as an elephant does. But he has an exceptionally alert sense of power, and he is very aware of

menace. When I was jet-lagged, I could read my condition in how he acted—whether he was maternal or
dodgy, amused or respectful.

I remember he said when I saw him, "Well, are you
ready for the madness?"

Here in the country, my moods are more settled than
they ever were in the city; it seems at first that there are
fewer stimuli to jog or tug at them, but really it is that
they are propelled differently. Energy functions differently among the trees. In the city, nothing is quite settled, ever. And other people's suffering, other people's
deaths, become unbearable. When I read the literature
on AIDS or walk the streets, I start to lose it; grief is
everywhere. In the country, flesh is grass, and the grasses
are settling into autumn. My bed is in a bay of five large,
mullioned windows, and the million leaves of the nearby
trees are struggling to dance. Of course, at this time of
year, they and I are all dying together. I hear the country-
side silence—it's something I can permit here—as focused on death. Getting into that mood is like going to
church or spending the day in the wind, with the steep
views and the hawks, and vultures, hovering. Two weeks
ago, Ellen and I saw flying very, very low, barely above our

heads on the country road, a young owl, head forward, beak faintly gleaming.

At one time I was interested in bird-watching, and I noticed that when I saw a bird for the first time I couldn't really see it, because I had no formal arrangement, no sense of pattern, for it. I couldn't remember it clearly, either. But once I identified the bird, the drawings in bird books and my own sense of order arranged the image and made it clearer to me, and I never forgot it. From then on I could see the bird in two ways—as the fresh, unpatterned vision and the patterned one. Well, seeing death nearby is very like the first way of seeing.

My agent, Deborah Karl, was up here yesterday and nagged Ellen a bit about her keeping a journal: I *think* Ellen's interest is piqued. (I am about to digress yet again.) Often the children and old friends call her and ask her what is going on and how I am, and I am mostly too tired to talk. But she is becoming trained in giving succinct reports, which might make up part of a journal. Still, unless I tell her to leave me in peace, she is with me almost every minute, not entirely watchfully, but nearly in the full emotional-psychological regalia of our years together, ready to fight or talk or to putter around and keep me from reading in order to prove how enticing she is and that I still care. I think she is most melancholy about my death when we lie side by side downstairs, on the two small couches in the bay, or in the bed up here, in the matching bay above the one below, and we read, side by side among the windows. What makes her sad is that the physical electricity and the competition, me turning pages at a faster, more snobbish rate than she can manage, and the verbal exchanges leading up to a touch of some kind have been exchanged for a gentle pathos, a quite remarkable but useless sweetness. This uselessness leads to weird little bursts of quite remarkable, but inactive, happiness. Actually, it is difficult to convey how deeply satisfying and *unrestless*, how vastly *monumental* and even baroque such domestic moments are when they are final and no longer part of a marital dialogue that is concerned with days and weeks, with the future.

This writing is a strain, and Ellen notices and protests that I should stop. She says that nothing matters but my comfort; that we have time or that we have no time for this sort of business—each of those statements means the same thing, I notice. Sometimes I stop, but sometimes I insist on going on, the man in charge. I exist. I matter *now*. She realizes the writing is an anodyne, the glancing and faintly radiant immediacy of the language. I am rough-edged with emotion—with indescribable unstillness—and I move in a sequence of moments that has no corollary.

The future is my estate. The fortune which I am leaving to this one and that one is to make room for them by my leaving. I am Harold Brodkey. (I am jealous even of my own name now, of the literal letters in print; it is a mild jealousy but it sweeps through me and, for a second or two, I don't know quite what to do with the rhythmic heat of it.)

Much of the time I do nothing. I lie in bed or on the porch. I stare at death, and death stares at me.

Late Winter 1994

My second *New Yorker* essay on the subject of my dying has just appeared. Barry still wishes I hadn't been so public. He doesn't want me to advise anyone else to go public. "Of all my patients, none, not one has had as good an experience," he says sternly. I haven't told him about the media attacks and unkind private comments. Or the indifference. (A big-time publisher wrote *Sorry to hear your bad news. If you ever get downtown, let's do lunch. I'll pay*.) Or the repeated experience of explaining AIDS and life expectancy (no one asks me, of course, how it is transmitted) and the simple moral collapse when such

sessions are over. After all, Barry had warned me that if
I made my condition public, the condition would become
the overt center of my life. I had told him that it was
therapeutic not to lie. That truth is a form of caress.
That lying is, among other things, conservative. We
quarreled about this on several visits, while he stuck
pencils and pens into the pocket of his white smock.

The overwhelmingly powerful thrust of bourgeois life
is to lie, is to hide things. A house, an office, is a stage
set. I think that much of what is hidden is chosen arbitrarily, family by family, person by person. Having
secrets and confessing them is what *deep* attachments
are about. Telling the truth is never wholly recommended, however. And now this. You might live longer
with AIDS than you're supposed to, medically speaking,
by not telling anyone you have it. Or at least that is one
theory. (But then maybe it's true of life in general that
you live partly by not letting others kill you, which is
hard, isn't it—all that swiveling to disarm antagonism?)
With AIDS, one is told, assuming the stress of public
excoriation on top of the stress of the disease itself—
which is, if you will, a state of precariousness beyond
belief—is probably unwise. People sometimes speak of
AIDS speeding up or slowing down based on these
external factors. If you lie and deny that you are ill, the

lying helps you live—helps you keep fighting. Of course, the lying means you have to put up a front, the stage set. The only other approach is to become an activist; you become ruthless in a way and you continue to live a while longer. I see now why Barry recommended secrecy so ardently (ardently for him), and said the only reason for going public is if you intend to be an activist, to serve in the war.

I don't want to die a politic liar, though I would prefer that to being a martyr, if one had a choice. I think all of us focus on the "survivors," or on the statistics through which their experiences become visible to us, and hope to be like them. But how do you measure the impact of truth against the impact of lying? So far, little has been found to indicate exactly what sort of person will be a survivor. Or rather, you will be a survivor by living, by being still on your feet at the funerals of others.

I'd rather be open about AIDS and scoff at public humiliation than feel the real humiliation of lying. I'd rather try to make this a death as much like any other as I can. Culture aims toward death, no matter what it says. (I also believe "sexual scandal" is an American universal, or nearly so.) I like the way the people in Barry's office and in the X-ray rooms downstairs smile openly at

me now and don't whisper. They ask me in a straightforward way how I am and comment on how I've gained
weight. These are the casual yet not so casual kind-
nesses that go with having this thing.

More and more as the months pass, I think Ellen needs a
territory for her omnipotence, a place where she can be
kind or fierce or merciful, as the final, uncontradicted
law; and where her cynicism and somewhat cold judgments can be petty (as mine can be) and kept hidden—
where they do not emerge as crimes-against-others. She
hates herself, I think, for not being an earner or a fighter
in the world. She tends to have no mercy on herself. She
is a mix of study and virtue. Sometimes she wants to be
rescued by another person. She can be amazingly selfish
in terms of ignoring another's guilt; she laughs and
turns away—that is her form of passing judgment. Her
wit and her estimates of people are unsentimental, but
she plays—very dangerously—with totalities. She is
technically as-if blind; she stares and lightly, breathingly
labors, blinded and unjudgmental. And she can be as-if
superhuman. She is with me, and I have seen her like
that with her children and the grandchildren and her
mother and sister. I have never been so trustingly close
to anyone since my real mother died.

I might say, "I'm not blaming myself—I haven't the energy to blame myself," and still she knows the complete mess of it all; knows, too, that though death has receded for a while, life won't come to take its place. Yet she has an entirely different notion of illness. She uses a mix of submission and discipline, with escape—with making a clear bolt for it—openly in mind all the while.

I remember one night, oh, maybe a few weeks after leaving the hospital last spring, when I had started feeling sort of better a little earlier than usual—at eight o'clock or thereabouts—and we were in the living room holding hands and watching television, she said, for the first time since we learned I had AIDS, "Do you love me?"

I turned to her, looked her in the face, and said something on the order of, Does that possibly matter now? And: "Ellen, I feel too disgusting, too subhuman to talk about *love*. And I've told you: I feel everything is occurring in a flat world, without dimension, without future, without color. Obviously I care about what you do. Obviously I love and admire you. But I am an object of charity."

The above may have been five speeches, with me serious, then teasing, then apologetically aware of my diminishing state and her locally omnipotent state. And with me gasping. And, in a way, reaching for power.

"Will you kiss me?" she said,

"Ellen, I'm filthy with AIDS. I have viruses crawling in me, hideous—hideous wrigglers. I smell to high heaven. I don't want to kiss anyone . . ."

"I've been bathing you. You don't smell." Then she tried another line of connection between her world and mine: "Tell me you love me."

"Why? Do you think I'm dying? You think we'd better have a full farewell now?"

"No. Of course not. I just want to know. I want you to tell me."

"Because of the AIDS? Because I'm so sick?" (The *because* being a way of hiding *in spite of*.)

"I just want to know."

"Of course I love you. So what? Love won't inspire the white cells." She was trying to cure me.

"Shhh, I know that," she said. I could feel her knowledge in me like a small, clear, delicate motion of the air, a response to the shame and apology in me. She moved closer. "Don't be difficult."

Ellen never teases and never persists; it's not her style. So this was strange, giddy-making. I felt pushed and prodded.

It didn't matter if she pretended I was sexy. The hollowness and grayness were embarrassingly clear. I joked about it—"I'm a dead man," I said. I spoke in very slow motion, and with what sympathy I could piece together for myself leaving without wanting to and for her being left behind: "I love you. I always loved you."

We could each of us measure the feverish deadness in me. We can feel each other's thoughts, the betrayals, the infidelities of attention, or what is worse, the absence of betrayals, of infidelities, except for my robust interest in death.

Within the sincerity of dependence, the full personality—with all its faulty construction and limited abilities—sooner or later rebels: it wants to be touched and known. There started up in me small flickerings of ego and of teasing her. These stirrings of mischief and of a refusal to be apologetic meant I believed her—and Barry—that I mattered, that I was not quite dead. The course and conduct of the illness, the various rashes and other symptoms, how I looked, the lack of focus in my face—all of it might have driven me mad with nervous fear and self-concern, but I judged my condition by watching her. And by teasing her. We hadn't had time to be this innocent with each other since I began publishing books. We hadn't had a time with so little ugliness in it.

The degree of public engagement was pleasant

enough or was an unpleasantry. Problems were all around in the shadows, in the corners of the room—problems about money and what some people were saying about me and doing to us, and whether the anomalies in my lungs were cancerous or cryptococcal or harmless. Meanwhile, we had our moments together. They occurred throughout the day but came to a climax of sorts each evening as we lay side by side and held hands and watched television, with one of us saying, "This is really OK, right? I'm not imagining it?"

The other would say, "No, you're not imagining it. I feel OK too."

"I feel really shitty, but actually—uh, you understand?—I haven't often been this happy," I said one evening. I felt shitty physically, but I was happy underneath. Or perhaps it was that I was happy, floatingly, on top, over the burning pits of illness. Comfortable. At home.

"I know. It's so strange," Ellen said. "I'd give it up in a minute for your health." She laughed a little. She leaned over and kissed me. "This is really terrible," she said in her omnipotent angel voice. "This is really terrible," she said in her omnipotent mother voice. "Tell me that you love me," she said in her lonely, ordinary, wounded, woman's voice.

A worrisome noise in my chest. The noise has to do with the pleura, some kind of infection roughly in the family of pleurisy. I go to see Barry, who thinks he might want to insert a needle between the ribs and make various other tests. I tell him we should not struggle to find out what it is. We wait awhile. The noise goes away. I go back. "Let me listen to your chest," he says. "Let's do an X ray."

"Christ, if it's gone, why be so nosy? You are really nosy."

"You *had* something in there. I want to be sure."

If Barry ever loses an argument to me, he will probably lose the rest of his hair.

I am lying diagonally among twists of linen sheeting in an enormous bed in a shuttered room under a giant glass chandelier glimmering complicatedly. I am in an apartment near San Tomà, with motionless white curtains masking the shuttered windows. I hear the warbles, coos, flutters of birds outside the shutters and the sounds of the reconstruction of the Casa Goldoni. Workmen's shouts, children, a dog. I hear the fluffing rise and shifting fall or slap of water in the small *rio* at the foot of the building wall, my bedroom wall. The room shakes lightly with the strange, pervasive vibrations of the traffic on the Grand Canal.

It is April and the start of my second year as an AIDS patient. I am in Venice at the invitation of Michael Naumann, my German publisher, to celebrate the release, in Germany, of my Venice novel, *Profane Friendship*. I am in Venice, but the sensation is that I wake in a box of consciousness of my own breath—without enthusiasm yet with wryly comic relief at not being dead, at not waking with a scream. I am very weak and fragile, and I find everything to be odd. Illness makes me shy; being ill is like the experience of public nakedness in dreams. In addition to AIDS, or in conjunction with it, I have bronchitis from the bad air on the plane during the flight here. Venice has been rainy and cold, and then hot; when I go out, I hear coughing all over the city.

10:15 A.M. My friend Giovanni Alliata-Cini's gesture in the *calle*, when we unexpectedly meet: he takes my hand in both of his and holds it and warms it. A deeply affecting death knell.

10:45 A.M. At a *traghetto* landing, in extraordinary, uncontaminated, assaultive light, as bright as if the sky held tiny particles of sharp-edged, gleaming glass, a bright, transparent glass dust. In this cutting light, the colors of the gardens and the colors of the buildings and the water in the Grand Canal do not disappear in glare or grow pale but take on a weird practical aura of being dressed up, brushed, and polished—the very distances in the view are polished. But not in the shade. There the water is dull, dirtyish, dark gray-green, and the stones show every crack. The dressed-up quality and the run-down quality observed together create an atmosphere of intimacy—perhaps one should say an extremely intimate reality.

Out on the choppy Canalazzo, among the *vaporetti* and scows and barges and the pretty *motoscafi*, the black ferries, called *traghetti*—which are rather plump open gondolas without seats, with one boatman at the bow and one at the stern poling twistingly and much more quickly than the regular *gondolieri* do—carry their erect, lightly swaying passengers standing very close to one another. Dressed in business clothes and carrying briefcases or portfolios; or in jeans and carrying schoolbooks; or in proper skirts and blouses, bearing string bags of vegetables and flowers in rolls of paper; or in work clothes, with tools in their arms or boxes balanced on their heads—these figures in a silent, polite clump are carried in the crowded craft over the water and its heaving reflections. It is very pictorial like Charon and a helper, carrying a clump of the newly dead to hell, a mystery of city existence, those lives swaying in the dark boat against a backdrop of *palazzi* and water traffic.

Six or seven Frenchmen and women of modest demeanor—not young, not well-dressed—came briskly along the *calle*, pushing wheelchairs in which were young-ish, twisted-up people, two of them breathing loudly and presenting distorted faces and looking enraged and/or sullen. A third, with a lifted clawlike hand, looked mur-derous. But the look was a viewer's misapprehension about retardation and deformity—about something child-like and perhaps truly innocent, although a real rage may have been there. They all seemed caged in special virtue, in special suffering, morally irresistible. (One time, driv-ing through Indiana, Ellen and I came upon a town that had a locally famous institution for people who required special care. These people worked around the town in stores and gas stations, and everyone adjusted to them. An ordinary townsman told me that it had once been a religious town but no longer trusted religion—because of Vietnam, he said. The townspeople had apparently replaced religion with devotion to the goodness and suf-fering of the slightly mad, the ill-since-birth, and the retarded. Everyone in the town seemed to me incontro-vertibly good.)

This *traghetto* landing is not far from the railroad sta-tion. Often, as soon as people disembark here, they break into an all-out run up the narrow *calle*.

A *traghetto* is efficient and rides lightly on the water

but is not stable, and it costs only five hundred lire, or a third of a dollar—the cheapest form of gondola ride in the city. Wind among the tallish *palazzi* adds swirls to the current and to traffic-churned waves and blows on the clumped people as on a clumsy sail. An anemometer whirls atop a metal rod on the dock. I have seen people in wheelchairs on *traghetti* but only one at a time and only ordinary people, not those caged in specialness: I have seen the *traghetto* men take a folded wheelchair and unfold it on the *traghetto* while an ill man hobbled into the boat on his wife's arm and then sat in the chair, the wind blowing his hair while he held his hat in his lap.

The *traghetto* men are mostly polite but standoffish, except toward one another; they display their warmth and solidity and amusement with one another. They are not forward like *gondolieri*, at least in my experience. They prefer not to be helpful. But sometimes they are. I have never seen one of them address a woman on the boat itself, but I have seen them be forward in the *calli* and in the bars. They inherit their rights to the *traghetto* crossing. They are as independent-seeming as Charon or as ranchers in American Westerns. They take frequent breaks, so seven or eight of them work here, keeping two *traghetti* in motion throughout the day.

The French pushed the wheelchairs into a tangle among those waiting for the *traghetto* and those disembarking from one—that is, they expected to board as a matter of course. One of the younger *traghetto* men waved them away. The *traghetto* men drink from morning on; they hold it well; but they are freed inside their day-long drunkenness. They are windblown and sunstruck, moderately tired, and somewhat drunk.

The oldest *traghetto* man, probably my age, showed his stolen and controlled drunkenness more than the younger man did. He hurried over to the French to get them out of the way. I doubt that he spoke to the point: he was allusive, artful, charming, intimate. One of the guardians, a woman, gave an affronted cry, a human gull, a cry of argument, of reproach. The French, the guardians of the angelic crippled, were stiff with rebuke at his heartlessness. He was pointing down the canal, to where, twenty-five yards away (though you would have to walk inland and then out to the canal again to reach it), there was a *vaporetto* stop. (Such stops have ramps, and each *vaporetto* has a central open space, where you often see people in wheelchairs.) During this episode, my own physical weakness caused me to unfocus and refocus. Also, there was the wind, and the space between me and the French. The perpetual children in the wheelchairs were caught in currents of thighs and midsections as foot traffic moved toward the boats or inland. The French were blocking most of the passage. The Italians dexterously wriggled past while accepting the circumstances of the others' being there, of there being a difficulty.

The French, observing the reality, lined the wheelchairs next to a railing on this portion of the *calle cum fondamenta*. This maneuver was performed with great deftness. There they stayed, forming a bank and narrowing the passage for perhaps ten minutes, until the guardians abruptly set off single file, pushing the chairs, heading inland like a line of cavalry, moving very quickly away from this submetaphysical corner of un-universal Venice.

11:10 A.M. Talk. Gossip. Conversation. In a hired boat. In our conferred stardom, out on the broad canal in the lightly explosive light, we experience illumination itself, but it is blinding and private: vision becomes recessive. The eyes recede under the brows, behind one's sunglasses, making one a sun-dweller, an Italian, of a kind. Ellen and I tell our friend Naumann about the French and the wheelchairs. We sit forward in the white *motoscafo*, near the boatman, who has a degree of pallor and the worn skin of a mainland Venetian working only part-time in Venice, outdoors. We enter the city's eccentric, expensive water labyrinth. Now we are a point of focus, an element in the sub-immortal picture. People filing into a *traghetto* look at us as do those on a full *vaporetto* and those at windows in the *palazzi*, or on the stone banks of the canal. We talk and chug past the lovely and worn and irregular jumble of decorative windows and columns and stones and marble ornament— we ruffle the green, restless mirror of the water. The Istrian stone of the city shines in this light. Architectural patterns tower around us in the beautiful Venetian visibility. Venice seems to be only its surviving beauty, such as it now is, a structure of appearances without a secret reality. . . . Of course, it still has secrets, but they are minor ones. I cannot recall a conversation in Venice that did not start with the topic of Venice. Or, one, this trip, in which the next remarks were not about my having AIDS. Then about Ellen's health. And state of mind. Then . . . but modern conversation—even when shouted over the noise of the motor in bright sunlight, with the boat chauffeur standing there—has a curious quality of occurring in a parenthesis that will be lost inside the machinery of any attempted biography or replication.

In Berlin and Paris and New York and Milan, the gossip and news-giving go on by phone and fax every morning—exchanging the real stories of everything. And at dinners. At lunch. In private conversation, face-to-face, this is merely a form of intimacy, trust, respect of a kind.

But, as public statements, the remarks, the voices, become scabrous. Naumann and Ellen and I *talk;* we use our actual opinions, our best information—real stories about Venice, New York, Berlin. But the real story of my death, the real nature of Ellen's and my relationship is private, is not to be historicized, not to be noted. Not yet.

History is a scandal, as are life and death.

I am dying . . . Venice is dying . . . The century is dying . . . The imbecile certitudes of the last three-quarters century are dying. The best journalism of the last half century has been leftist; which means that human nature was shown as innocent, as decent at the beginning and end of each story. A phantasmagoria, a piety, that idea—an abdication of reality, an infinite condescension toward anything less than absolute power. Similarly, novels were fantastic—like spaceships that as a matter of course left this world. The real was forbidden.

Naumann says I am a *monstre sacré*, but I am not so famous. I am aware of the monstrosity of my own will and of individual will in anyone. Imprison people and their lives become monstrous. Set people free and they become monstrous. We must change our notions.

Our boatman did not at first remember San Sebastiano, the parish church of Veronese, but he accepted my description, spoken in a gasping baby's Italian. He half remembered then. For fifteen years, Veronese painted in that small church. He grew wise, so to speak—an aging mixture of cold and hot. We turned from the brilliant sunlight and the restless water of the Grand Canal into the shadow of a smaller canal leading to the Giudecca. I feel unwell restlessly, resentfully. Just before we turn into the wide Giudecca, I look up and see the people there on the *fondamenta* as taller than they are and foreshortened, like figures in a ceiling fresco. One group of young men, each of them oversized in a shapeless fashion—not exercised-looking, but strong, rough-haired, and loud, in tight clothes—were pushing and shouldering their way along, drinking as they strutted, and photographing themselves with a video camera. Fini people, the boatman said, Fascists.

We pulled out into the Guidecca, and they shrank in the distance. The current Italian Fascists are not quite *neo*-Fascists, as they claim; they are forced by Italian law to deny any connection to Mussolinian doctrines and deeds, but Mussolini's granddaughter is one of the leaders of their party. Not out in the *calli* but at the soccer stadium, in that national privacy, they shout anti-Semitic slogans and wave anti-Semitic placards. Apparently, it is possible to attend a game safely only if you sit on the expensive side of the stadium—as in England. Violence is the will of the people.

From the center of the Giudecca, across the water, in a distant haze, refineries and industrial chimneys on the heavily built-up mainland are visible. The industrial plant is outdated and no longer represents much in the way of money. It represents votes and redundant and unhappy workers. The local megalopolis stretches to the head of the Adriatic and around as far as Trieste. In the other direction, it runs through Padua and on to Mantua. Trieste and the Veneto and Venice and these other districts all together make up an urban conglomeration like the one around San Francisco Bay and down the peninsula.

The day smells of salt and sun and of the onset of blood. But Venice itself, in its watery surround, is parenthetical to immediate violence. The guardians of the churches and other places we visited demonstrated degrees of seduction and difficulty of temper toward foreigners. One, a usually very quiet man—Ellen and I see him frequently when we are in Venice—was in a state of explosive rage because someone had spilled Coca-Cola on a marble floor *nella chiesa*, "in the church." But it was not a consecrated church; it was the chapel of San Giorgio degli Schiavoni—St. George of the Slavs. Violence is the will of the people, off and on, and Venice was always racist.

8:00 P.M. Dinner at the Monaco, on the raft-terrace,

sunset striping the sky with softly hazed bands of sulfur-polluted yellows and stained pinks and grayish mauves. The two domes of the Salute were backlit. The Dogana gleamed. The factories, the activities in Mestre and Santa Margherita, the flames of the refineries had been visible from the boat earlier, but the wind rather delicately carried a touch of pollution, chemical nastiness. The winds blew it here lightly, strange acidic elements in the Venice mixture of curling cool-and-damp and the African hot-and-dry. Boats crossing the Bacino were beginning to turn on their lights. Year by year, there is less variety among the boats. Venice, as it ages into being a museum of itself, grows simpler. But it is unlikely it can ever have the quality of true simplicity. It is elaboration itself. How I wish for the causeway and the railway to be dismantled, and for Venice to be cut off from the mainland and the lagoon restored to swamp, for the city's filled-in and paved canals to be returned to water, for Venice to be unpedestrian, isolated, impractical, wholly itself and unlike the rest of the world.

At the large table on the raft-terrace sit Naumann and Ellen and Fritz Raddatz, a critic for *Die Zeit*, who has admired my new novel in his column. A Berliner by birth, he now lives in Hamburg, and is here in Venice so that we can meet. He is en route to give a speech and a seminar in Rome. My German translator, Angela Praesent, who lives in southern France, is here, and Volker Hage, of *Der Speigel*, is here; he is a model figure of the New Germany. Francesca De Pol, a Venetian, who works for the Consorzio Venezia Nuova, which commissioned a book from me, is here.

I may be the central figure of the dinner, but everywhere in the world—even in Paris—condescension flows from critics toward writers; the point of the critic is to demonstrate mastery in the contemporary moment. He or she has an army of readers, phalanxes literally. But a writer is alone, is a sacrificed beast and madman (or madwoman) and fool. Or is someone dying or drunken. This "condescension" is sometimes delicately or heavily lightened by admiration. Or by envy and rage. Or by sympathy. But a writer has no legions, no phalanxes in a direct sense, only a "name," a perfume, a reputation.

As the light around us altered, as shadows and glare played idly, and as-if jeeringly erased vast stretches of famous cityscape, Raddatz addressed me as *cher maître* in a tone that meant that we were celebrating a private success, one that hadn't happened publicly yet, that might not happen. (Some books emerge as significant only over time and exist uneasily in the present moment as intellectual and political and economic facts. One can avoid this, can write differently.)

Raddatz is a man my age and has great energy—

German energy, unlike American or Italian vigor, Böhm, as opposed to Bernstein or Giulini. I have never been energetic or active—strong, yes, at one time, but never adventurous or quick. Sitting in a chair on a raft-terrace is my sort of adventure. It is odd to me how aesthetic intelligence and a sense of—what to call it— journalistic and immediate power can seem grotesque with bravery and self-assertion, a madness of the normal, of normalcy.

Still, one might say at the table, among the people there, women and men—including the maître d' overseeing everything and present as well—that blind surges of power disordered the moments; reputations and imputed events and events-to-come quivered and rippled foreignly like the surfaces of the moving and darkening water at our feet. Power and the mix of cultures and genders and private stories were tactfully shaped in my favor—perhaps out of pity, perhaps out of respect.

One hardly expects *truth* anymore in anything, and Venice is, in any case, a city in which truth was used with a degree of fantasy to achieve a potent and salable insobriety—so human. It is a monument to fantasy-made-actual, insolently pictorial and mostly festive, self-hypnotically.

I will not attempt to do the voices or judge the talk or the moods on the raft-terrace.

It grew darker, and across the flickering water the lights bloomed on the facade of Palladio's Redentore. That Palladian facade has as an aesthetic quality, an un-Venetian and as-if-final, brooding stillness. It was built to honor the end of a plague. It testifies also to the wretched capitalism of the survivors—the city was already dying then; the facade is something of a tomb-stone for accident and evil, for ruin and death as if they will not occur again. . . .

I can't remember ever wishing life and death had a perceptible, known, over-all meaning. When I was a child, I wished only for life, a little more of it, or much more of it. In the first torments of adolescence, I wished for a little less of it, for peace from it and its dangers. I think of breath as noisy and containing a kind of reason or meaning, as in the half prayer of *Let me breathe*. I think of the mind as rebellious and made of interruptions and demands for the ideal and private flights; it is dangerous to love minds, even one's own. I have accepted since child-hood the transience of everything, including meaning— poor orphan that I was. The arrival and departure of significance was something I was used to, not in the sense that the significance appears once and disappears for good, but in the sense that impure versions of it recur, as my party-loving parents came and went, dressed and left the house and returned: they return in memory still. This hasn't changed with illness. Death has a transient significance for me, one that changes. My sense of it changes, too—the imagery, the shock along the nerves, the fear (or terror) behind the breastbone. I tend to treat myself as if I were a nervous dog, a schnauzer, say. *It's all right,* I say to myself, *It's all right.* Sometimes it seems to me my blood, my bones, my nerves, my mind, my heart whisper to one another but not to me: I feel like the dissolving parent of the parts of me that there are. I would like to endow a small *chiesa* in Venice, to be called the Church of St. Death and the Ease of Leaving True Meaning Behind.

At some point, the waiters cranked out a brown-and-white striped awning, so that we were in a canvas-topped room beside the water. Some kinds of frivolity, like some kinds of selfish insistence, have an earnestness, a hidden skeleton of grace—I do not really understand this.

By ten-thirty I was exhausted, and, too tired for a *motoscafo*, I went with Ellen onto a *vaporetto*. We entered the cube of its lights. The *vaporetto* in a small surround of bright water in the middle of the dark held the casual fellowship of a public vehicle at night. It chug-chugged up the Canalazzo. I leaned on Ellen, who supported my weight as we went riding past the darkened or lit facades of the palaces of the Grand Canal.

I would have liked to give sketches of Ellen and Naumann and the others who came to Venice to see us, but I don't think sketches of actual people can be managed by the ill. One has a sense specialized by illness of other people as vivid and active and insensible. But they are outside the cage and still exist in the wild, complete with a future, those people, those lives. For me, now, real faces, real presences, are not decorated by needs or interests of mine. I think it would be an extraordinary intrusion, a trespass, to describe a real face coldly and what I see written there, death or triumph, hatred and disappointment, madness or escape from madness, curiosity, hidden, lonely love, appetite, and ferocity and wit, or blindness. I prefer to be truthful and clear-eyed about imaginary faces. Or ones belonging to the dead. I have always half-known that the narrator of *The Runaway Soul* would have to die in some sense to himself before he could describe himself lucidly, cruelly, simply.

It starts in my sleep, a partly dreamed memory of being young and about to wake to the life of a young man. This morning I was playing basketball with Michael Jordan, and I was as big as he was, or bigger. What a mass of roles, or personae, is mixed in when one is ill, alongside the self-loathing and self-protection, the recurring simplicity and the terror. My identity is as a raft skidding or gliding, borne on a flux of feelings and frights, including the morning's delusion (which lasts ten minutes sometimes) of being young and whole.

I took the responsibility for keeping my parents alive—I did it, all told, for seven years, first my father, then both, then my mother for a while, not steadily, but as best I could. (My memory of that time is that I was conceited in a rather contingent and hopeful way. I was evasive and not so smart all in all, and I was without conscious ambition; I was waiting to have a fate thrust upon me, as it surely would have been if the war had continued.) The money I earned as a tutor and as an usher in the ballpark paid for a cleaning woman. And my real father sent me money which I used for household expenses. We had a kind of little civilization going in the apartment. I mostly tried to keep everything limited to one set of meanings, the nonphysical, nonscreaming, nonsexual set; the life-and-death and we-love-each-other set. They tore it all down periodically, like drunkards. And I think my eluding them was the compass reading that guided them and persuaded them to live. Some people fight toward a terrestrial ideal, toward an ideal love, feeling that it was promised them and that the promise was withheld.

Then, I killed Joe Brodkey. But I didn't know—scientifically—it would kill him to talk to him with intelligence and finality. I stood up and leaned against the bureau and he lay on my bed, and I said he could not touch me anymore at all, not even a handshake, unless he *behaved*. Murder is always an experiment in reality by the poor, proud mind. Rhetorically and emotionally, it was enough to condemn him; he writhed and groaned and glared at me. He turned his face to the wall, telling me I was a cold fish—because I would not sex around with him. He was lecherous and strange.

About abuse, being abused: it is such an immense subject that the problem if one tries to think about it and talk about it is how to keep the narrative and descriptions and judgments within some sort of boundary.

At the end of the period in which I pursued the "truth" of these matters, I met a schoolteacher named Charles Yordy. Charlie was ten, twelve years younger than I was. I met him in 1970 or thereabouts at the baths; I used to go to homosexual baths, usually in the afternoon, when they were quiet. At those times I could have, in relation to society, a de facto invisibility,

secrecy, privacy. Charlie had been adopted, and he was
nursing his dying father. He was crazy—crazy and intelligent and often inspired. He was half-Polish, half-
Italian, reared by backwoods, small-town Wasps in
Pennsylvania. He was an officer in his chapter of the
teachers' union. He was also a sexual genius, really,
class-conscious and inferior and angry, but a full vessel,
alive and insanely restless. He faced me with a mix of
adoration and utter rage.

It isn't that I saw myself in him. No. But for the first
time I glimpsed bits, portions of my story with Joe
Brodkey in another person's life. I began to write differently. The first story was called "Story in an Almost
Classical Mode" and the second was called "Innocence."
Both were about the autonomy of women and each
rested on my having made my escape from Joe Brodkey,
even if incompletely.

Charlie had no particular regard for his adoptive parents that I could see, but he was loyal in his physical
servitude to them. He had a straightforward air but
muddied blue eyes that told you nothing he did not want
you to know. He spoke with a series of highly stylized
gazes. He was very sharply observant was Charlie. He
was the one who pointed out to me that all of Dick
Avedon's fashion photos were of Dick himself, while the

serious photographs were of *the other*. (This is a cliché now but it was new then.)

He moved in with me—actually two men lived with me during those years. The other one, Douglas, was completely different: Danish-German by descent, six-foot-five, very blond, with a manner of someone very young. I would fuck them occasionally, usually one by one, and do "romantic" things. The sexual stuff was gravy; what I needed was protection while I worked and tried to make sense of the past and of other lives. Writing keeps you humble but it also locks you in self-involvement. There were bouts of actual destruction, but for a while anyway, they did protect me while I wrote. And I amused them when they were depressed and introduced them to clever people.

Charlie's love was always angry and involved courage and a sense of being cheated. Nobody but needy little kids were entirely real to him. Kids got to him. He was one of the most successful teachers ever at the ritzy suburban school he taught at. No kid could escape his sympathy. Or escape being educated. But he rarely liked his students' parents—rarely liked people. He had no interest in growing up. He died of AIDS. I think he was the one who gave it to me.

Years later, when he was dying, he left his lover and

came back to New York to be near Ellen and me. He was strangely docile and reasonable, hard-working in terms of courage despite the pain and the diseases. He went into the hospital at the end. He wanted to talk to me. He did not say he liked me or that he had enjoyed knowing me or that I was, I don't know, someone he had spent years with; he asked me about my sense of God. Then, the next day, he told me that he had seen God in a vision.

The last day of his life he telephoned early, as I was getting dressed to go to the hospital to see him. He said he was in the intensive care unit and that he'd figured out how to give up—that he'd had a strong sense of God in a blistering flash of light that ended and then that didn't end somehow.

Then, instead of saying good-bye or anything like that, he said, "I'm as smart as you are now," and hung up.

Living on for a while, waking in the morning, sitting here and writing are part of the peculiar equation that the more strength I have, the more fear pushes at me and I have to work or dance or pray. I am stronger for the moment, which is maddening, since it means that I am only stronger for the moment; did you know that logic and intelligence depend on a future? For me logic has become terrifyingly pure, a mere exercise as out-of-date as hawking.

The fear moves in me and has no hard outline. It surrounds me with strange whispers of electricity and a sense of expulsion, of my being launched into the light— or the dark. Fear shouldn't be thought of unphysically. It shouldn't be packed into a *word*. I am not so immediately in the hands of death, yet I am closer and closer.

Sometimes I can still sleep it off, my fear. My dreams are gentle now even when they are about being mugged, robbed and knocked down, even when I am pressing my car key into a bit of yielding earth. But often in the afternoons I wake after a nap with an awful sense of its being over and that it never meant much; I never had a life. The valuable sweetness and the hard work are infected by the fact of death: they no longer seem to have been so wonderful, but they are all I had. And then I want to be comforted. I want my old, unthreatening forms of silence, and comedy-and-cowardice. I want breath and stories and the world.

VICTIM SONG

Oh, I have practiced victim art,
AIDS-spattered and insolent in heart—

I have put the hearse before the cart,
oh la-di-ra di-ra di-ra . . .

I must mask myself in a burlap vizard
and tape my mouth and cement my gizzard,
so I can't whisper, " 'Tis hard, 'tis hard,"
oh la-di-ra di-ra di-ra . . .

I will lie among the liberal leaves
and rot gently while the red wind grieves
and the prizes go to the neocon thieves,
oh la-di-ra di-ra di-ra . . .

When, finally, I went off to college, my mother's sister Ida yelled and raged at me that I was killing Doris by leaving her. I said to Ida, "It's time you lived with her if you care so goddamn much."

Doris had a special hospital maquillage. A small-town beauty, she remained good-looking to the end. I bought her a silver compact at Shreve, Crump & Low in Boston, when I was at college, and a French bed jacket. She whispered to me her two last requests, one of which was for morphine and the other for me to learn to pick up my shirts and not treat women as servants. Before that, she had asked that I not blame her for the awful parts of the past and that I remember my real mother as she, Doris, had promised my mother I would.

I have missed my mother, Ceil, all my life—her physical size, her mind, her odor, a small-town odor with a faint smell of dust in it. Her heat had a coolness in it.

I was told stories, chiefly by Doris, of Ceil's journey to this country from Russia, after her having been raped or abused in the revolutions of 1905 and 1917, and of life in the small town, much smaller than Alton, where Ceil lived. But the operative fragments for me were, first, that I knew her—*She held you and would not put you down*—and, second, that she disappeared. All children are afraid when their mother leaves the house that she will not return. I dreamed of this throughout my childhood (and dream of it now that I am the one who is about to leave and not return), because one day, when I was a year and a half old, it happened—or rather, to be exact, it began to happen. Her disappearance revealed itself day by day—it was not a single moment, not even a single moment of acknowledgment or of despair; it was a thing that moved from minute to minute and hour to hour among other events. A mystery.

SUMMER 1994

This morning, on what may be one of my last visits to our country house, when I drove into town to get the paper, I saw a man who was my height and built something like me, but he was about thirty-five years old, and healthy. For a second it was as if I had been split down the middle by an ax. I bit on darkness . . . the slain man bites darkness and falls to the something-something earth, Homer says.

Ellen looks well today, even radiant. It is the fresh air and the garden. From my study window, I can see her working; her light vigor and dexterity and strength are reassuring, but also a bit shocking to me. How alive she is. Nothing quite moves me like the sight of health, like a healthy motion—my head jerks around: *Look at that,* I cry inwardly, *Look how healthy* . . .

The garden is hers now. It wanders between stone walls that we built to guard a steep slope. Most of this garden is at eye level, and so it is like a living painting or series of pictures of plants but struck with active, not painted, light. One of the reasons for making such a garden was that someone my size could work in most of it without kneeling and without intruding on the plants. I have a green thumb but I am clumsy, and I have noticed that some plants when they bloom seem to have a Darwinian pride that needs space and, as it were, privacy in order to be at their best and most seductive to bees and humming birds (and even the wind) in the fat light, after the thin light of winter.

Ellen is thin and adroit, and she works with a young gardener named Liza McCrae, who is as dextrous and who is also quite lovely and quite independent—it is in her posture, which is as fierce as that of any blooming plant using sunlight and sight lines and lifting its flowers to where they might be seen. She is fiercer than a plant, of course, but almost as quiet and nearly as silent. She is young. My wife is twice Liza's age but is beautiful, as beautiful as Liza, and is spindly-fierce in a similar style, but she is sadder than Liza and more overtly protective and a bit more lost in the vast spaces and corridors of fate and time, where Liza is pure defiance so far.

They are amazing creatures in the sunlight, neither ever admitting to tiredness or thirst, each one as fine-grained and as fine-nerved as the plants themselves; ruthless, quick, and deft, they dig and hoe and pluck and pinch. It seems to me they leave no footprints even in the softest soil, no footprints, no crushed leaves, no broken stalks.

Sometimes they take a break and talk to each other, one standing, one sitting, or both sitting in their gardening hats. If they laugh, it is quiet and slightly distant, rather like the sounds the garden makes, or the sounds one imagines anemones when they conceive or roses might make in the early summer air.

I am enraptured by the sight of women in a garden . . .

The memories of gardens, the green embodiments of the ideas that gardens carry out—ideas of happiness, toy vistas, sculpted light—are something I use to ease bad hours. I can recall happiness in a garden so strongly it fills me with a suffused delight, a blush of pleasure.

We are quite happy today, really. It's an hour-by-hour thing. I don't know what anything costs Ellen anymore. When I look at her, when I study her face-to-face, she masks everything but sympathy—and waiting. Well, she shows affection and amusement. And astonishment sometimes. I can make her cry quite easily by saying, "Don't ask me about the attic fan: do it the way you want it." With the implication, of course, that I won't be here. The book is always closing.

The figures of my blood tests have taken the expected swing downward, and unless the tests are in error, my run of comparative luck is over. I am able to work but not with great lucidity. I don't seem to be ill yet—it's been two years without an infection and I have been spared the wasting syndrome—but I am more fatigued again and sicker from the medicines.

Death is a bore. But life isn't very interesting either. I must say I expected death to glimmer with meaning, but it doesn't. It's just there. I don't feel particularly alone or condemned or unfairly treated, but I do think about suicide a lot because it is so boring to be ill, rather like being trapped in an Updike novel. I must say I despise living if it can't be done on my terms.

With AIDS you often get very, very bad dandruff. I have it. How to convey this sense of one's *self* shredding? And tension makes my eyes water; my stomach, the upper part near the throat, fills with acid. I choke on the stupidity. Nausea starts in, to grind away and throb. All deaths are ironic, cancers, heart attacks, all of them. They hardly suit what the man or woman was except as ironic comment.

I don't want any human gesture of solidarity. I feel quite human anyway, infinitely human, which is to say merely human, and I don't feel the need for physical reassurance. I find the silence of God to be very beautiful, even when the silence is directed at me. I like to be alone, me and the walls. I do what I do, I think what I think, and to hell with the rest of it, the rest of you; you don't actually exist for me anyway—you're all myths in my head. Like Doris at the end, you play a role. I have a sense of performance now in every aspect of living.

The truth is that I have lost my sense of people. I mean, this is what actually happens when you remove some of the common falsification of a hopeless, terminal situation, some of the pretense of being gods on a Roman ceiling.

At the beginning, more than two years ago, I thought it a matter of etiquette and of courtesy to be publicly brave about this illness, but it has become more difficult as time passes. Ego has resurfaced and so has bad temper. Death and pain are like a grisly conspiracy, hirelings for the moment, bosses-to-be during the overthrows and revolutions. I can smell them, my constituency. I am as cranky and snobbish as Coriolanus. I now try to make use of the disease, and I say things such as, "Don't bother me with that—I'm *dying*, for God's sake." The drawback of this is it has the effect of making one a further object of curiosity and opportunity, as someone who is dying along a continuum of worsening circumstances. People pretty much are structured to treat you according to how well you can protect yourself; that is, if you have visibly little strength, you become someone to rob—of dignity, of money, or what-have-you. This isn't always conscious. Often, though, it is.

It seems to be an almost automatic tic in certain folk, men and women, rich and poor, to grab at triumph and to exercise self-assertion at others' expense. In the beginning, when we discovered I had AIDS, Ellen and I found it difficult to lie about it, and it was a relief to be candid and open. Now my candor about AIDS is chiefly an objection to the world itself, a sort of challenge: *Let's see how you are going to lie to me now.* And nearly everyone does lie, the most intelligent and kind (I am inundated by tales of survival and by assurances that I will survive) as well as the most ignorant and unkind. I knew that Barry had been afraid for me, that he encouraged lying as a way to make things easier for the person with AIDS. I had foreseen only some of what would happen.

I regret having been so polite in the past. I'd like to

trample on at least a dozen people. Maybe I will live long enough to do just that before I waste away to the point where I can't trample on a goose feather. Anyway, I have been in bed, in the fetal position, for two weeks. I wish I were young. I am sick of leaves and fresh air. Nature doesn't seem serious enough, or rather it seems *too* serious on the death front.

It's hard to know, when one has invented a term ironically, whether it is already full-fledged jargon—at any rate, I am nowadays exceedingly fond of the term "stress management." Stress management means nearly total irresponsibility: a sleeping pill every night, endless television, answering mail only when I feel worldly or sociable. It's an ancient adolescence, and a male-diva thing . . . *Look, I'm dying* . . .

The procession of pills: this morning two Advil, one 3TC, one AZT, one Paxil, one Mycobutin, and on and on, and last night a pentamidine treatment while I was

drenched in night sweats. It is the bodily weakness
and my own sense of ignorance that form the pit of
blackness and fill me with impatient dread. The needle
has replaced the kiss. Death and I are head-to-head
in a total collision, pure and mutual distaste. Death does
not want someone who tastes of medication and is
bloated and blurred, fat and pale—and dandruffy; I am
physically intellectual, finally. But death's acquisitive
instincts will win. I feel death as dirt closing over me.

Some people I once knew very well have not written
or phoned since I became ill. Perhaps they do not want
to intrude. Perhaps I have been and am even more irritating than I used to suspect. It is difficult under such
circumstances, really, to wish one had loved any of them
more or been more agreeable. One wishes *they* had loved
more lastingly, more percipiently. Or with more forgiveness. (One wishes anything and everything, depending
on the hour and the degree of unease that the proximity
of death brings.)

We have put our country house up for sale, and Ellen
has brought much of the furniture back to the apartment. So, everywhere I look now are old, pretty things,
bits of things. The other day I stumbled and knocked a
wooden raven off its shelf, and its beak struck me and
drew blood, unsafe blood. "But what does it mean?" I
asked Ellen. She is still strong and still wants us to spend

time together—she is collecting minutes. I see an *Orlando*-ish quality in her now: she is father and mother and wife and husband and daughter and son; she is herself and the me-of-the-vanished-years.

Somewhere in American naval history is an admiral who said to his second-in-command, *Fire when ready, Gridley. . . .*

October 25, 1995: It is my birthday. And for the first time in my adult life, it matters to me that the age I have reached is a specific number. I am sixty-five years old, but it is not so much that I am sixty-five as the idea of birth and near old age and now death. I do not know at what rate of speed I am moving toward my death. The doctors cannot tell me—the only hard medical fact with AIDS is death. The hard social fact is the suffering. One approaches the end of consciousness—or the end of consciousness approaches one—and strange alterations of the self occur: a hope of cure, a half-belief in treatments that could extend life. (By a year, two years? Three years is so vast a time, one thinks of life as being extended indefinitely if one can hope to live three more years.) The less luck one has, the stronger is one's new conviction in one's luck. This while the doctors back away. They have nothing more to offer. They conserve their energies and the hospital's medical resources, but what it feels like is being locked out of the house when I was six years old. The experience is closer to the early, angrier descriptions of AIDS than I had expected it would be for me or others after all these years.

I am sleeping without a detritus of dreams or symbols now, without images, not lions or tigers, not flowers or light, not Jesus or Moses—but a few memories, chiefly of childhood, perhaps because of the night sweats, which I have all day long sometimes. I am rolling down the grassy hill behind the house in Alton. It is twilight. Dark shapes flit in the air—bats, I say now, like a schoolchild answering a question in class. And the birdsong! The pre-DDT birdsong: I had no idea I missed it so harshly. Sing! Chitter! A train travels on the tracks below the cliff, below the limestone bluff. Chug-a-chug, chuff-chuff. The grown-ups sit in those heavy wooden lawn chairs of the 1930s: so still, so handsome. And I, a pudgy child who will not use words yet, this soon after his mother's death, in high-sided shoes and white socks, I am shouting, yelling, in my own sort of birdsong, yelling and grumbling as I roll; stones and pebbles bite into my ribs. I am magnifying my size with the sound I make. Faster and faster I go, then either my father stops me or I curl up against a tree trunk, I'm not sure which.

The change in momentum changed everything, how the light darkened and had a name, like dusk; how the trees and faces emerged and could be named. I remember feeling large from the adventure but small as well, factually small. And because I was in my own mind no one thing, large or small or boy or son of this household, I remember the dreamlikeness of being no one, of being lifted and of being of no important weight. The smells, the grass, my father's shirt—they were more important than I was. I was no one and nothing, about to be devoured by sleep.

I take 300 milligrams of AZT and 300 milligrams of 3TC daily, and my T-cell count is over 100 again. This might be delusive, but I am grateful. I inhale pentamidine about every three weeks. I take between fifteen and twenty pills a day. The cost is astronomical, and so are the fees of the lawyers even when they shave them out of friendship. Tina Brown of *The New Yorker* and Deborah Karl said from the start they would protect us. I don't know if you can understand what such warriors' support means when you are helpless. Kindness always conveys a great deal of meaning about the universe, but perhaps it matters more, shines more brightly, in relation to this disease than to any other at the moment. I think it is because this disease makes an even greater mockery of everything one was before—mentally and physically, socially and erotically, emotionally and politically.

I wish someone would find a cure. I really don't want to die this way. (And I would like to feel my death had some meaning and was not an accident and that it belonged to me and not to those who talk about it.) But at the same time I have to confess that I haven't a great deal to complain about. I often want to go along the street, chanting *Save me, save me, save me,* but I do not do that, partly because almost every act of charity and compassion brings me some meaning and ease. My grandson Harper said, *Are you sick?* And I said, *Yes,* and then he changed the subject. When the visit ended, he made a point of telling me that he liked me quite a lot. I like him quite a lot. He was going off with his other grandfather to Kenya and South Africa for a few weeks. I told him to whisper my name to the grass when he was in Africa, and he very unsolemnly repeated my words and said he would do it.

Today I cannot find anything in my life to be proud of— love or courage or acts of generosity. Or my writing. My life has been mostly error. Error and crap. It seems to have been a load of crap to have been alive. Everything in language goes dead, in a morbid Rockettes march.

I have not been able to work for six weeks, but when I could I was working on a memoir piece about Frank O'Hara, who introduced me to the work of Pollock and Rothko. Today I was thinking about my first sight of a drip Pollock: the paint hardly dry, and the madness and vitality, the quivering beauty, the shock, the immense, immense freshness.

I remember Chartres in 1949 before the stained glass was restored. No one I had spoken to and nothing I'd read had prepared me for the delicacy of the colors, the pale blue, a sky blue really, and the yellow. The transcendent theater of the nave while the light outside changed moment to moment—clouds blowing over—and the colors brightening or darkening in revolving whorls inside the long, slanted beams of lady-light. I had never been *inside* a work of genius before.

I have started to die again. I made a recovery with new pills, but then collapsed. I am what is called a disconnector: some measurements of my condition are favorable and others are not, but they move in ways unrelated to one another when they should move conjointly.

I sometimes see in the mirror the strange rearrangement of an adopted child's face in preparation for entering his new household.

I find operatic arias to be very moving now—showy and subtly coarse, technically elaborate, lengthy, embarrassingly detailed and impolitic, un-American, and beyond the hemming and hawing of dialogue.

My dreams are mostly of vacations again and have a still-sweet quality; they even comment on the sweetness of the air and light in the strange, new place where I am a tourist. It is a maybe cheapened version of paradise. The dreams usually end in a gentle drowning, and then I wake.

I ought to have dinner. I haven't eaten or taken my pills—just a little suicide. I mostly live because of Ellen, although I might put on a show if any of the grandchildren were in the apartment. It is unbelievably strange to live when things are *over*, when things are done with. Poor Kundera. It is the unbearable lightness of not-being. What do you suppose an embrace of mine would be worth now?

In New York one lives in the moment rather more than Socrates advised, so that at a party or alone in your room it will always be difficult to guess at the long-term worth of anything. When I first started coming to New York, I was in college at Harvard. This was six years after the end of the Second World War. New York didn't glitter then. There were no reflecting glass buildings but, rather, stone buildings that looked stiff-sided and had smallish windows that caught sun rays and glinted at twilight: rows of corseted, sequined buildings. Driving through the streets in a convertible owned by a school friend's very rich mother, one was presented with a series of towering perspectives leaping up and fleeing backward like some very high stone-and-brick wake from the passage of one's head. Advertising flowed past, billboards and neon and window signs: an invitation to the end of loneliness. New York was raunchy with words. It was menacing and lovely, the foursquare perspectives trailing down the fat avenues, which were transformed in the dimming blue light of the dissolving workday. Overwhelming beauty and carelessness, the city then— one of the wonders of the world.

New York was the capital of American sexuality, the one place in America where you could get laid with some degree of sophistication, and so Peggy Guggenheim and André Breton had come here during the war, whereas Thomas Mann, who was shy, and Igor Stravinsky, who was pious, had gone to Los Angeles, which is the best place for voyeurs. I was always crazy about New York, dependent on it, scared of it—well, it *is* dangerous—but beyond that there was the pressure of being young and of not yet having done work you really liked, trademark work, breakthrough work. The trouble with the city's invitation was that you were aware you might not be able to manage: you might drown, you might fall off the train, whatever metaphor you preferred, before you did anything interesting. You would have wasted your life. One worked hard or not at all, and tried to withstand the constant demolishing judgment. One watched people scavenge for phrases in other people's talk—that hunt for ideas which is, sometimes, like picking up dead birds. One witnessed the reverse of glamour—that everyone is jealous. It is not a joke, the great clang of New York. It is the sound of brassy people at the party, at all parties, pimping and doing favors and threatening and making gassy public statements and being modest and blackmailing and having dinner and going on later. (It was said you could get anyone to be disliked in New York merely by praising that person to someone nervous and competitive.) Literary talk in New York often announced itself as the best talk in America. People would say, "Harold, you are hearing the best in America tonight." It would be a cutthroat monologue, disposable with in passing, practiced with a certain carelessness in regard to honesty. But then truth was not the issue, as it almost never is in New York.

Learning to write: I remember the sheer seriousness of the first acquisition of some sort of public ability, learning something; learning also the fragility of mental acquisition, the despair as this new thing slipped from my mental grasp. You become rigid in your attempt to hold the acquisition; if it stays, or more exactly, if it recurs, others join to it. Perhaps you build your daily life around this oddity. You don't let it go when people talk to you or when fucking or when people tease your deepest attention. *You are a cold person,* people say of this trait.

I am an addict of language, of storytelling and of journalism. I read, not frenziedly anymore, but constantly. I long to love other people's words, other people for their words, their ideas. I do dearly love conversation as a self-conscious, slightly or greatly social climber's art. I love to talk, and I prefer it by a large amount if nothing depends on the talk, not money or sex or invitations—just the talk, like experiments in pure science, or as a funny mix of chemical and electrical investigation that has to be immediately comprehensible—and immediately comprehended—and in which no one can dominate, and dexterity really is all.

Telephoning is a wonderful waste of mind, the vocal do-jiggers, all of it lost as soon as said. And behold the little faxes. The little faxes devour the tender gripes.

As someone who is ill, I feel I have only dubious rights to interrupt anyone else's life, and I try to control access to my own time. I do not like to watch people wrestle with the fact of who I am and with my death and what it means to them, but if one is open about having the disease, such reactions and intrusions are inevitable. I did not really expect to live this long. I do not think I am reasonable, but I do not care if I am reasonable or not.

I have tried some of the new drugs. There is an as-yet-untried one called saquinavir and to get it I entered a lottery for patients with very low T-cell counts, a salvage drawing, I think it's called. I won a lottery once before, in the fourth grade. This time it appears there will be a delay: a special hospital board has been set up to review the lottery and the allotment of the drug—I think it is mostly to prevent doctors from being trapped by sympathy. Or self-importance. There is a rumor that the drug, a protease inhibitor, besides being the weakest of the PI's, is difficult to manufacture. There may well be a shortage and a delay, which means we could all die before we try it anyway.

For me, neurotic (if that word still has meaning) or not, illness had never been a useful reality, never a landscape (or kingdom) of increased sensitivity or heightened storytelling. I remember thinking a year or so ago that if my strength went it would not be possible to think, to write. I have no gift for sickness. And I am not graceful in my dependence.

I did apologize to Ellen once. I said I was sorry, really sorry, to do this to her, to be so much work, and after a rather long pause, she said, "Harold, you were always this much work. All that is different is that I give you meals in bed and I cry when you are in pain. But you were always work."

And I am still writing, as you see. I am practicing making entries in my journal, recording my passage into nonexistence. This identity, this mind, this particular cast of speech, is nearly over.

Late Fall 1995

I am at the end of the list of AIDS drugs to take. I wake frightened now; it is a strange form of fright— geometric, limited, final.

Being ill like this combines shock—*this time I will die*—with a pain and agony that are unfamiliar, that wrench me out of myself. It is like visiting one's funeral, like visiting loss in its purest and most monumental form, this wild darkness, which is not only unknown but which one cannot enter as oneself. Now one belongs entirely to nature, to time: identity was a game. It isn't cruel what happens next, it is merely a form of being caught. Memory, so complete and clear or so evasive, has to be ended, has to be put aside, as if one were leaving a chapel and bringing the prayer to an end in one's head. It is death that goes down to the center of the earth, the great burial church the earth is, and then to the curved ends of the universe, as light is said to do.

Call it the pit, the melodramatic pit: the bottomless danger in the world is bottomed with blood and the end of consciousness. Yet I don't wake angry or angrily prepared to fight or to accuse. (Somehow I was always short of rage. I had a ferocity and will but without rage. I often thought men stank of rage; it is why I preferred women, and homosexuals.) I awake with a not entirely sickened knowledge that I am merely young again and in a funny way at peace, an observer who is aware of time's chariot, aware that the last metamorphosis has occurred.

I am in an adolescence in reverse, as mysterious as the first, except that this time I feel it as a decay of the odds that I might live for a while, that I can sleep it off. And as an alteration of language: I can't say *I will see you this summer.* I can't live without pain, and the strength I draw on throughout the day is Ellen's. At times I cannot entirely believe I ever was alive, that I ever was another self, and wrote—and loved or failed to love. I do not really understand this erasure. Oh, I can comprehend a shutting down, a great power replacing me with someone else (and with silence), but this inability to have an identity in the face of death—I don't believe I ever saw this written about in all the death scenes I have read or in all the descriptions of old age. It is curious how my life has tumbled to this point, how my memories no longer apply to the body in which my words are formed.

Perhaps you could say I did very little with my life, but the *douceur*, if that is the word, Tallyrand's word, was overwhelming. Painful and light-struck and wonderful.

I have thousands of opinions still—but that is down from millions—and, as always, I know nothing.

I don't know if the darkness is growing inward or if I am dissolving, softly exploding outward, into constituent bits in other existences: micro-existence. I am sensible of the velocity of the moments, and entering the part of my head alert to the motion of the world I am aware that life was never perfect, never absolute. This bestows contentment, even a fearlessness. Separation, detachment, death. I look upon another's insistence on the merits of his or her life—duties, intellect, accomplishment—and see that most of it is nonsense. And me, hell, I am a genius or I am a fraud, or—as I really think—I am possessed by voices and events from the earliest edge of memory and have never existed except as an Illinois front yard where these things play themselves out over and over again until I die.

It bothers me that I won't live to see the end of the century, because, when I was young, in St. Louis, I remember saying to Marilyn, my sister by adoption, that that was how long I wanted to live: seventy years. And then to see the celebration. I remember the real light in the room; I say real because it is not dream light. Marilyn is very pretty, with a bit of self-display, and chubby, and she does not ever want to be old like Gramma. If she is alive, she would be in her seventies now; perhaps I would not recognize her on the street.

I asked everyone—I was six or seven years old—I mean everyone, the children at school, the teachers, women in the cafeteria, the parents of other children: How long do you want to live? I suppose the secret to the question was: What do you enjoy? Do you enjoy living? Would you try to go on living under any circumstances?

To the end of the century, I said when I was asked. Well, I won't make it.

True stories, autobiographical stories, like some novels, begin long ago, before the acts in the account, before the birth of some of the people in the tale. So an autobiography about death should include, in my case, an account of European Jewry and of Russian and Jewish events—pogroms and flights and murders and the revolution that drove my mother to come here. (A family like mine, of rabbis, trailing across forty centuries, is a web of copulations involving half the world and its genetic traces, such that I, wandering in the paragraphs of myself, come upon shadows on Nuremburg, Hamburg, St. Petersburg.) So, too, I should write an invocation to America, to Illinois, to *corners* of the world, and to immigration, to nomadism, to women's pride, to lecheries, and, in some cases, to cautions. I should do a riff on the issues of social class as they combine with passionate belief and self-definition, a cadenza about those people who insist categorically that they, not society, not fixed notions, will define who they are. My life, my work, my feelings, my death reside with them.

My own shadows, the light of New York, sometimes become too much now; I pull the shades. I have been drawing spaceships for my grandsons.

I feel very well, and for a week now, as part of some mysterious cycle, I have felt very happy. Also, today, for no particular reason, I am enormously conceited about my writing. Everyone is more interested in my death. I cannot be bothered with my death except as it concerns my books. When I write it out like this, it is a pose, but

inside me, it is very real, very firm, this state, very firm
for a while. Actually, all my states are now very precarious, just as if I were dancing except that the motion is
that of time, or of my time, and it is this time that might
stumble and fall, might seem to—that is what I mean by
precarious.

The world still seems far away. And I hear each
moment whisper as it slides along. And yet I am happy—
even overexcited, quite foolish. But *happy*. It seems very
strange to think one could enjoy one's death. Ellen has
begun to laugh at this phenomenon. We know we are
absurd, but what can we do? We are happy.

Me, my literary reputation is mostly abroad, but I am
anchored here in New York. I can't think of any other
place I'd rather die than here. I would like to do it in
bed, looking out my window. The exasperation, discom-
fort, sheer physical and mental danger here are more
interesting to me than the comfort anywhere else. I lie
nested at the window, from which I can see midtown and
its changing parade of towers and lights; birds flying
past cast shadows on me, my face, my chest.

I can't change the past, and I don't think I would. I
don't expect to be understood. I like what I've written,
the stories and two novels. If I had to give up what I've
written in order to be clear of this disease, I wouldn't
do it.

One may be tired of the world—tired of the prayer-makers, the poem-makers, whose rituals are distracting and human and pleasant but worse than irritating because they have no reality—while reality itself remains very dear. One wants glimpses of the real. God is an immensity, while this disease, this death, which is in me, this small, tightly defined pedestrian event, is merely real, without miracle—or instruction. I am standing on an unmoored raft, a punt moving on the flexing, flowing face of a river. It is precarious. The unknowing, the taut balance, the jolts and the instability spread in widening ripples through all my thoughts. Peace? There was never any in the world. But in the pliable water, under the sky, unmoored, I am traveling now and hearing myself laugh, at first with nerves and then with genuine amazement. It is all around me.